ADVANCE PRAISE FOR

The Carbon Charter

During a time when municipalities are both insolvent
and crumbling under the weight of short-sighted
assumptions, Godo brings forth an attainable green
vision for municipal leaders to create effective change
with. We know that the majority of our municipal
leaders have acted responsibly and seek to embrace
our challenging future; here is one of the keys to
that future. Godo Stoyke raises the bar again.

~ Joey Hundert, social entrepreneur, Philadelphia, PA

The *Carbon Charter* is an invaluable resource
for local governments that want to lower
their carbon footprint. It is an excellent source of
best practices, and is organized in a manner that
facilitates technology transfer. Godo Stoyke has
developed a wonderful how-to guide based
on the leading carbon reducing efforts
in the world from local and state governments.

~ Roger Duncan, Austin Energy

The roots of the *Carbon Charter* are growing in
hope and in the fertile compost of communities all over
the world creating bold, local solutions. Godo Stoyke
gives the challenge of carbon reduction the flavor of
a treasure hunt. The invitation to join is irresistible.

~ Rob Harlan, Executive Director
Solar Energy Society of Canada — Northern Alberta Chapter

PRAISE FOR GODO STOYKE'S

The Carbon Buster's Home Energy Handbook

This book offers real solutions for reducing our
energy use and helping our environment.

~ *Doug Anderson, ENERGY STAR program,*
US Environmental Protection Agency

For all of us who want to reduce our environmental
impact and save money, here is the invaluable, practical
resource we've been looking for. If you are concerned about
global warming, rising fuel costs, or the world we will leave
our grandkids, read this book, and tell your friends.

~ *Alexis Karolides, Rocky Mountain Institute*

At last, a book written in plain English that guides you
step by step through the best choices to make for reducing
both energy costs and carbon emissions at a family level.

~ *Richard Freudenberger, publisher*, BackHome Magazine

This book is a dream come true for anyone who wants to
reduce their carbon emissions in the most cost-effective way.

~ *Guy Dauncey, author of* The Climate Challenge:
101 Solutions to Global Climate Change

THE CARBON CHARTER

blueprint for a carbon free future

Godo Stoyke

NEW SOCIETY PUBLISHERS

Cataloging in Publication Data:
A catalog record for this publication is available from the National Library of Canada.

Copyright © 2009 by Godo Stoyke.
All rights reserved.

Cover design by Diane McIntosh. Image: Inge Hardmann, Oceanview Photography
Printed in Canada. First printing June 2009.

New Society Publishers acknowledges the support of the Government of Canada through the Book Publishing Industry Development Program (BPIDP) for our publishing activities.

Paperback ISBN: 978-0-86571-634-6

Inquiries regarding requests to reprint all or part of *The Carbon Charter* should be addressed to New Society Publishers at the address below.

To order directly from the publishers, please call toll-free (North America) 1-800-567-6772, or order online at www.newsociety.com

Any other inquiries can be directed by mail to:
New Society Publishers
P.O. Box 189, Gabriola Island, BC V0R 1X0, Canada
(250) 247-9737

Disclaimer
Though we believe the information in this book to be accurate, the author and the publisher make no warranty of any kind, expressed or implied, with regard to the performance of any procedures or products described herein. The author and publisher shall not be liable in any event for incidental or consequential damages in connection with, or arising out of, the use of these procedures or products.

Carbon Busters® is a registered trademark of Carbon Busters Inc. Other trademarks or registered trademarks are the property of their respective owners.

Financial self-disclosure: The author of this book owns stock in Ballard Power Systems Inc., a manufacturer of hydrogen fuel cells, and in Arise Technologies Corporation, a manufacturer of photovoltaic cells.
This book was written on a solar- and wind-powered energy-efficient MacBook Air.

New Society Publishers' mission is to publish books that contribute in fundamental ways to building an ecologically sustainable and just society, and to do so with the least possible impact on the environment, in a manner that models this vision. We are committed to doing this not just through education, but through action. This book is one step toward ending global deforestation and climate change. It is printed on Forest Stewardship Council-certified acid-free paper that is **100% post-consumer recycled** (100% old growth forest-free), processed chlorine free, and printed with vegetable-based, low-VOC inks, with covers produced using FSC-certified stock. Additionally, New Society purchases carbon offsets based on an annual audit, operating with a carbon-neutral footprint. For further information, or to browse our full list of books and purchase securely, visit our website at: www.newsociety.com

NEW SOCIETY PUBLISHERS
www.newsociety.com

Mixed Sources
Cert no. SW-COC-001271
© 1996 FSC
FSC

This book is dedicated to my brother,

Asmus Stoyke,

the best brother in the world

ACKNOWLEDGMENTS

FIRST I WOULD LIKE TO THANK THE WONDERFUL STAFF AT NEW Society Publishers (newsociety.com), especially Chris and Judith Plant (publishers), Ingrid Witvoet (editor) and Sue Custance (production manager) for their dedication and patience, Diane McIntosh (cover designer) for the awesome cover, Greg Green (book layout and design), as well as Ginny Miller and EJ Hurst for their marketing savvy. Special thanks to Michael Mundhenk (copyeditor) for many corrections and suggestions throughout the manuscript.

Next, I would like to thank the talented staff at Carbon Busters for their numerous hours of meticulous background research for this book, especially Eckhart Stoyke, Richard Krause, Shanthu Mano, and Erich Welz. Thanks to carbon buster and graphic designer Denise Dahl for her eternal cheerfulness, her dedication to design, and her creation of icons, cover ideas, and numerous illustrations. Thanks to Guy Dauncey (earthfuture.com) for giving me access to an early draft of his 2009 book *The Great Climate Challenge: 101 Solutions to Global Warming* and for permission to quote from his book *Cancer: 101 Solutions to a Preventable Epidemic.*

Companion Website and QuickLinks

For updates, free downloads, and updated links to original legislative and support documentation visit CarbonCharter.org or enter the short and convenient QuickLink URL for extra content.

char·ter (chär't_r) noun

1. declaration of fundamental values and principles
2. a statement of the scope, objectives and participants in a project

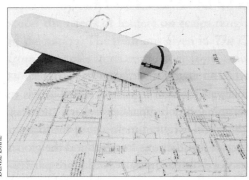

DENISE DAHL

THE STATE OF THE PLANET

IN 2000, KOFI ANAN, THEN SECRETARY GENERAL OF THE UNITED Nations, proposed the undertaking of the Millennium Ecosystem Assessment. It was cochaired by Robert T. Watson, Chief Scientist of the World Bank, and A.H. Zakri, Director of the Institute of Advanced Studies of the United Nations University. The four-year study was released in 2005 after the input of 1,360 experts from 95 countries. Its purpose was to assess the changes in ecosystems over the course of past decades and to project changes into the future. It is considered one of the largest studies of the Earth's natural systems ever undertaken.

Declining Ecosystem Services

"Nearly two thirds of the services provided by nature to humankind are found to be in decline worldwide. In effect, the benefits reaped from our engineering of the planet have been achieved by running down natural capital assets. In many cases, it is literally a matter of living on borrowed time."

~ Millennium Ecosystem Assessment, 2005

Some of the general recommendations put forth in the Millennium Ecosystem Assessment include the following:

- Remove subsidies to agriculture, fisheries, and energy sources that harm the environment.
- Encourage landowners to manage property in ways that enhance the supply of ecosystem services, such as carbon storage and the generation of fresh water.
- Protect more areas from development, especially in the oceans.[8]

"The challenge of reversing the degradation of ecosystems while meeting increasing demands for their services can be partially met under some scenarios that the MA [Millennium Ecosystem Assessment] has considered, but these involve significant changes in policies, institutions, and practices that are not currently under way."

~ Millennium Ecosystem Assessment, 2005[9]

The Value of Ecosystem Services

Ecosystems provide many valuable products that are traded in the marketplace. These include fish and other marine foodstuffs, timber, fibers, and terrestrial food.

GLEAM, YOKOHAMA, JAPAN, GNU FREE DOCUMENTATION LICENSE

FIGURE 2.6
The Biosphere II project demonstrated the difficulty and great cost of artificially providing ecological services for even a handful of people.

However, ecosystems also provide many services that are not traded in the marketplace. These include filtration of wastes and pollutants, regulation of the earth's climate, protection from extreme weather, floods, land slides, fire, and disease, even from tidal waves (for example, East

Indian mangrove forests), regeneration of clean air, water, and soil, and inspiration, recreation, spiritual sustenance, and support for a way of life.[7]

According to Amory Lovins, chief scientist of the resource efficiency think-tank Rocky Mountain Institute (rmi.org), "Biosphere 2" was a US$200 million experiment in the Arizona Desert about two decades ago, whose purpose it was to create an artificial environment that could support human life. However, even though a lot of good science went into the project and in spite of its staggering cost, the artificial environment was unable to provide many ecosystem services, such as breathable air for eight people, on a consistent basis (Figure 2.6).

"Even today's technology and knowledge can reduce considerably the human impact on ecosystems.

They are unlikely to be deployed fully, however, until ecosystem services cease to be perceived as free and limitless, and their full value is taken into account."

~ Millennium Ecosystem Assessment, 2005[9]

"Biosphere 1" (the Earth), on the other hand, provides this service for more than 6.7 billion people on a daily basis, for free.[10] Even though the service is free, economists have estimated its economic value. In 1997, a number of economists and ecologists examined the economic value of 17 ecosystem services for 16 biomes (large ecosystems that are climatically and geographically defined) and published the results in the respected scientific journal *Nature*. The scientists arrived at a minimum average estimated value for these 17 services and 16 biomes of US$33 trillion (US$33,000 billion) in 1997,

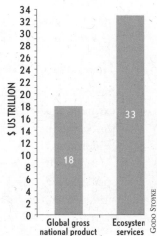

FIGURE 2.7
Value of 17 ecosystem services in 16 biomes vs. global gross national product in 1997 US$.[9]

GODO STOYKE

FIGURE 2.8
A comparison of the planetary ecological footprints over time (shorter is better). Around 1990, humans started exceeding the planet's carrying capacity.[12]

compared to a global gross national product of around US$18 trillion for that year (Figure 2.7).[11]

The economic value of ecosystem services provided by the planet to humanity—not currently accounted for in our economic system — has been estimated at US$33 trillion per year.[11]

When humans impose a new role onto an ecosystem or degrade the functioning of that ecosystem, they may be able to extract an economic benefit from this change, but when the loss of non-market ecosystem services is taken into account, this impairment can have a negative net benefit (Figures 2.8, 2.9, 2.10).

QuickLink: CarbonCharter.org/01

The Loss of Biodiversity

Next to climate change, the loss of global biodiversity through the extinction of species of plants, animals, and microorganisms is probably the other most serious global environmental threat (Figure 2.11).

While the slow loss of existing species and the creation of new species over very long periods of time is a natural process, the human-induced loss of species biodiversity is now estimated to be at 100 to 1,000 times the natural background rate.[8]

The International Union for Conservation of Nature (IUCN) is the world's main authority keeping track of the conservation status of plant and animal species, having representation from over 200 government and 800 non-government organizations and enlisting

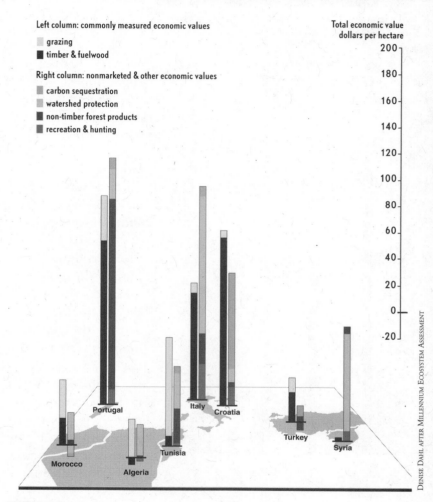

ANNUAL FLOW OF BENEFITS FROM FORESTS IN SELECTED COUNTRIES

Left column: commonly measured economic values

- grazing
- timber & fuelwood

Right column: nonmarketed & other economic values

- carbon sequestration
- watershed protection
- non-timber forest products
- recreation & hunting

Total economic value
dollars per hectare

FIGURE 2.9

A comparison of the measured and non-measured economic values of forest ecosystems in selected countries. The measured value (timber and grazing) is often lower than the non-measured value (carbon sequestration, watershed protection, non-timber forest products, recreation, and hunting). (Illustration after Millennium Ecosystem Assessment, 2005.)[9]

ECONOMIC BENEFITS UNDER ALTERNATE MANAGEMENT PRACTISES

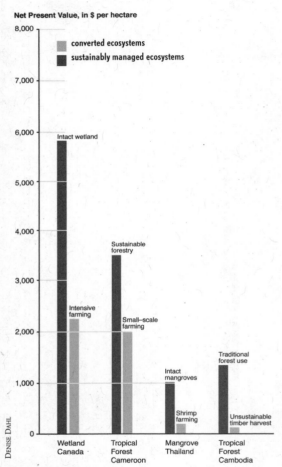

Net Present Value, in $ per hectare

over 10,000 volunteer scientists and experts from 140 countries.[13] The IUCN is currently monitoring 41,415 species on its Red List. In 2008, 16,306 of these (just under 40%) were reported to be threatened with extinction, an increase of 188 species in just one year (Figure 2.12). By 2008 a total of 785 species had already become extinct.[14]

It should be noted that the animal Red List, as is reasonable, is biased towards larger and vertebrate species, despite the fact that most of the planet's two million described species are arthropods (mostly insects). Research conducted in the tropics points to the highly endemic nature of many insect populations. It is

FIGURE 2.10
A comparison of market and non-market economic values of converted and non-converted ecosystems in selected countries. In each case, the non-converted value of the ecosystems exceeds the economic value of converted ecosystems. (Illustration after: Millennium Ecosystem Assessment, 2005.)[9]

therefore likely that a very large number of never classified arthropods have already become extinct, before even having become known to science.

Humans are now more populous than any other mammalian species on the planet (the common house mouse, *Mus musculus*, being the second most abundant).[15]

FIGURE 2.11
Next to climate change, loss of global biodiversity through the extinction of plant and animal species is probably the most serious global environmental threat (American Emerald Dragonfly, *Cordulia shurtleffi*).

CLIMATE CHANGE

The greenhouse effect is a natural phenomenon that makes life on earth possible by raising the planet's average temperature above freezing. Water vapor and carbon dioxide are two important naturally occurring greenhouse gases.

Concern about climate change is based on anthropogenic greenhouse gases, i.e., greenhouse gases that are being added to the atmosphere due to human activity. Of these, carbon dioxide is the most important, with 51% of net radiative forcing, followed by methane (17%), halocarbons (11%), and tropospheric ozone (11%). Current air pollution in the form of aerosols (especially sulphate aerosols) appears to have a significant cooling effect on the planet, partially offsetting global warming (Figure 2.13).[16] Nearly every country in the world has ratified the Kyoto

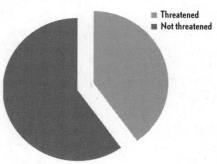

■ Threatened
■ Not threatened

FIGURE 2.12
Of the 41,415 species on the IUCN Red List of monitored species, 16,306 (39.4%) were threatened with extinction in 2007.[14]

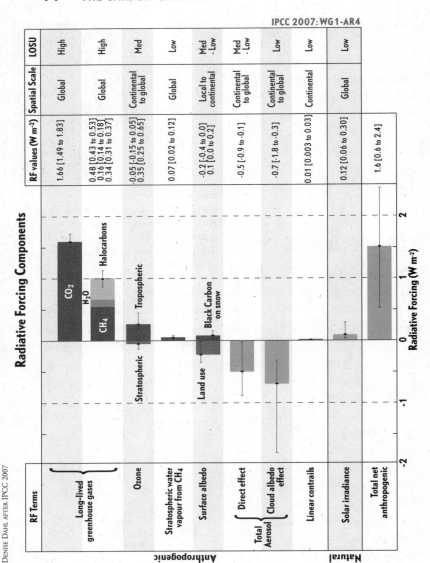

RF Terms		RF values (W m⁻²)	Spatial Scale	LOSU
Long-lived greenhouse gases	CO₂	1.66 [1.49 to 1.83]	Global	High
	N₂O / CH₄ / Halocarbons	0.48 [0.43 to 0.53] / 0.16 [0.14 to 0.18] / 0.34 [0.31 to 0.37]	Global	High
Ozone	Stratospheric / Tropospheric	-0.05 [-0.15 to 0.05] / 0.35 [0.25 to 0.65]	Continental to global	Med
Stratospheric water vapour from CH₄		0.07 [0.02 to 0.12]	Global	Low
Surface albedo	Land use / Black Carbon on snow	-0.2 [-0.4 to 0.0] / 0.1 [0.0 to 0.2]	Local to continental	Med -Low
Total Aerosol	Direct effect	-0.5 [-0.9 to -0.1]	Continental to global	Med -Low
	Cloud albedo effect	-0.7 [-1.8 to -0.3]	Continental to global	Low
Linear contrails		0.01 [0.003 to 0.03]	Continental	Low
Solar irradiance		0.12 [0.06 to 0.30]	Global	Low
Total net anthropogenic		1.6 [0.6 to 2.4]		

FIGURE 2.13
Relative importance of changes in anthropogenic and natural radiative forcing components.
(Illustration after IPCC 2007: WG1-AR4.)[16]

DENISE DAHL AFTER IPCC 2007

Protocol, a tiny but significant step towards reducing greenhouse gas emissions.

RESOURCES

The complete Intergovernmental Panel on Climate Change (IPCC) Fourth Assessment Report from 2007 (also known as AR4) is available in three volumes, free of charge, from the IPCC website:

- Volume I *The Physical Science Basis* at ipcc.ch/ipccreports/ ar4-wg1.htm
- Volume II *Impacts, Adaptation and Vulnerability* at ipcc.ch/ ipccreports/ar4-wg2.htm
- Volume III *Mitigation of Climate Change* at ipcc.ch/ipccre ports/ar4-wg3.htm

These volumes are also available in printed form from Cambridge University Press cambridge.org.

The *Synthesis Report* for policy makers can be found at ipcc.ch/pdf/assessment-report/ar4/syr/ar4_syr.pdf.

See also the section "You Want This by *When?*" on p. 27 for updates on rapid climate change.

QuickLink: CarbonCharter.org/02

"It's easy to predict the future, it's being right that's difficult."

~ Anonymous

FROM PEAK OIL TO PEAK SUSTAINABILITY
What is Peak Oil?

American geoscientist M. King Hubbert presented a paper at the 1956 meeting of the American Petroleum Institute where he predicted that overall petroleum production would peak in the United States between the late 1960s and the early 1970s. He based his prediction on his finding that regional oil production tended to follow a bell curve, typically declining at about the same rate at

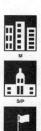

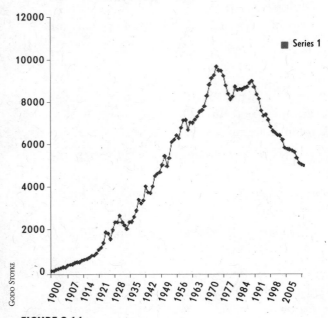

GODO STOYKE

FIGURE 2.14
US crude oil field production in thousands of barrels per day from 1900 to 2007, showing peak production in 1970 at 9,637 thousand barrels per day (2007 production: 5,064 thousand barrels per day).[20]

which production increased, after maximum production peaks. The prediction was widely ignored or even derided, but came true when US oil production peaked in 1970.[18] [19] The National Academy of Sciences accepted Hubbert's calculations on oil depletion and admitted that their own more optimistic estimates had been incorrect (Figure 2.14).[21]

Then, in 1998, Colin J. Campbell and Jean H. Laherrère published an article entitled "The End of Cheap Oil," in which they predicted that production of conventional oil would probably decline within 10 years. Others had already been writing about what later came to be commonly known as "Peak Oil," but since Campbell and Laherrère's article was published in the influential journal *Scientific American*, it received far wider notice.

Campbell and Laherrère pointed out that 80% of the oil produced in 1998 was from fields discovered before 1973 and that in the 1990s the rate of extraction outpaced the rate of new oil discovery by a factor of three to one. The authors stated that when production falls below demand, there may still be plenty of oil left, but that prices would rise significantly. Somewhat presciently, they added, "Barring a global recession, it seems most likely that world production of conventional oil will peak during the first decade of the 21st century."[18]

In this context, it is interesting to examine the "energy return on investment," or EROI, of oil and biofuel production (Figure 2.15). The energy return for oil dropped from a high of 100 barrels of oil equivalent (BOE) returned for every barrel invested in 1945, to 9 barrels for conventional oil and 3 barrels for tar sands (bitumen or oil sands) in 2008. For the tar sands, that represents a decline in EROI by a factor of over 30, indicating that we are beginning to scrape the "bottom of the barrel" with respect to energy returns. The increasing costs of oil exploration and recovery alone are likely to ensure that we will not return to pre-2005 prices for oil for any extended periods of time soon (barring, again, periods of extended global economic slowdown).

In one study, ethanol from corn was calculated to have an EROI of 0.7 to 1.8 — a range from a negative energy balance to a positive one.[22] A

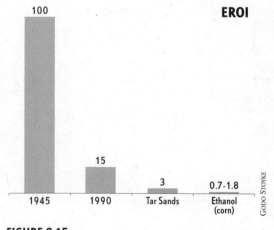

FIGURE 2.15
Energy return on investment (EROI) of oil production from 1945 to 2008, expressed in barrels of oil equivalent (BOE) returned over BOE invested, compared to ethanol from corn.[22, 23, 24]

number of studies indicate, though, that there are many options that would allow us to produce sustainable biofuels with high energy returns without jeopardizing food production. Even switch grass has already been replaced as a potential ethanol champion by the perennial grass *Miscanthus*, which in field trials showed over three times the dry yield per acre and year.[25] David Blume in *Alcohol Can Be a Gas! Fueling an Ethanol Revolution for the 21st Century* describes many sources for sustainable ethanol production, ranging from fodder beets and Jerusalem artichokes to non-agricultural sources such as cattails and marine algae, and even stale donuts (Figure 2.16).[26] A study by Dartmouth College researcher Lee Lynd and colleagues shows how we can move from an unsustainable food vs. fuel position that would require two and a half times the arable land in the US, to resource sufficiency in food *and* fuel with zero additional cropland requirements through integration of agricultural and transportation approaches and cellulosic ethanol production (Figure 2.17).

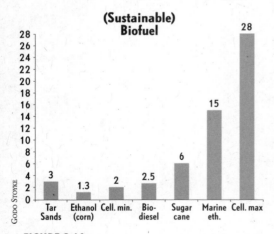

FIGURE 2.16
Energy return on investment (EROI) of biofuels, expressed in barrels of oil equivalent (BOE) returned over BOE invested, compared to oil from Alberta tar sands (bitumen sands). Cell. = cellulosic ethanol.[23, 24, 25, 26]

The US Government Energy Information Administration (EIA) conducted its own study in 2000 and concluded that the most likely date for Peak Oil was 2037, with a possible range from 2021 to 2112. This position was reaffirmed in 2004 and still appeared to be the official stance in 2008, though the EIA seems to be increasingly isolated in this opinion.[27]

The EIA's own numbers show that global oil

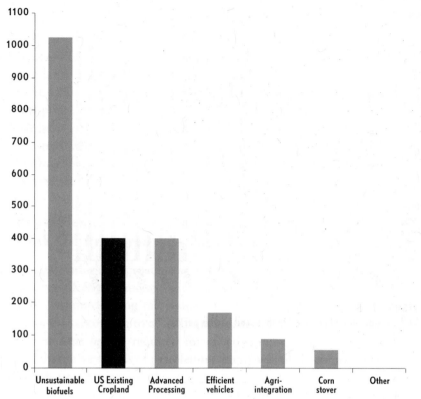

FIGURE 2.17
New land requirements in million acres (1 acre = 4,000 m2) to meet present US light- and heavy-duty vehicle energy demands through biofuels (after Lynd et al. 2007).[25]

production peaked in 2005 and has declined slightly since (Figure 2.18). Is this the beginning of Peak Oil or just a temporary reduction in extraction rates? One of the problems in determining Peak Oil is that it is generally only possible to determine the actual peak in retrospect.

However, the widening gap between increasing consumption and decreasing new discoveries does not bode well for low oil prices in the future (Figure 2.19). It seems clear that countries, municipalities, and economies that are less dependant on erratically

- Slide show of San Francisco Peak Oil Preparedness Task Force: sfgov.org/site/uploadedfiles/lafco/peak_oil_hearing_richard_hei nberg.ppt
- globalpublicmedia.com/sites/globalpublicmedia.com/files/ SFPeakOilTaskforce-Meeting1.pdf
- Book: Richard Heinberg. 2007. *Peak Everything: Waking Up to the Century of Declines*. New Society Publishers.
- The Association for the Study of Peak Oil and Gas — ASPO International: peakoil.net, ASPO USA: www.aspousa.org **QuickLink:** CarbonCharter.org/03

THE CLIMATE CODE

Stone Age

"The Stone Age did not end for lack of stone. The Oil Age will end long before the world runs out of oil."

> ‑ Attributed to a Saudi oil minister

THE CLIMATE CODE
Fire

SHORTLY AFTER MIDNIGHT ON SUNDAY, SEPTEMBER 2, 1666, A small fire started at the bakery of Thomas Farynor, baker to King Charles II, on Pudding Lane in the City of London. At one in the morning, a servant woke to find the house blazing from the fire. The baker and his family were trapped upstairs but managed to escape over the rooftops. However, a maidservant too afraid to try perished in the blaze. The fire leapt to the hay and feed piles in the yard of the Star Inn at Fish Street Hill. Most houses in London were built of dangerously flammable materials like wood and pitch (tar) and were separated only by narrow streets, and so the fire spread to the Inn. Strong winds carried sparks to the Church of St.

DENISE DAHL

FIGURE 3.1
The Great Fire of London of 1666 destroyed the homes of 90% of its inhabitants and provided the impetus for improved building materials, precursors of modern building fire codes.

Margaret and by eight in the morning the fire had spread halfway across London Bridge. By afternoon the fire turned into a raging firestorm, and by Sunday evening the streets were jammed with the carts and bundles of fleeing citizens. By Wednesday, September 5, 1666, 70,000 of the city's 80,000 inhabitants (nearly 90%) had lost their homes (Figure 3.1).[31, 32, 33, 34]

By 1680, London had established the "Fire Office," and the city was rebuilt with wider streets, open access to the river Thames, and buildings constructed of brick and stone, not wood. These measures were the precursors of modern fire codes, fire prevention codes, and fire safety codes. We also have building codes that ensure that buildings are structurally sound and healthy for occupants, safety codes to prevent accidents at work sites, and health codes for food production and handling, worker safety, and numerous other aspects of our lives.

The key to codes is their proactive, preventive nature; they make sure that we take action to prevent negative outcomes *before* they occur. These codes are vital to ensuring our health and safety, and we ignore them at our peril.

The Climate Code

There are electrical codes, gas codes, plumbing codes, emergency action codes, codes for public welfare, and even a code for fireworks displays.

However, climate change, the ultimate global disaster, is not covered in any code.

Not only is there no climate code, but some local building ordinances actively prohibit or prevent environmental and climate-critical technologies and processes. Examples include bans or restrictions on wind turbines and building-integrated photovoltaic (solar electric) systems, clothes lines, high permeability driveways (which reduce stormwater runoff, recharge aquifers, and reduce air conditioning loads), the use of greywater, and over prescribed lighting levels in buildings.

Not only do we need to reexamine all of our existing codes, from fire to building to safety to health, in the light of what is emerging as humanity's biggest health and safety issue, namely climate change, but we have to actively draft a comprehensive body of bylaws and ordinances that work proactively to reduce and — ultimately — reverse global climate change. In other words, we need a *Climate Code*. And we need a "climate hall," staffed by dedicated municipal workers who ensure that the climate code is taken as seriously as all other safety and emergency codes (Figure 3.2).

Starting Points

As the examples in the following chapters show, there are already numerous bylaws, initiatives, and pieces of legislation that lay the groundwork for communities to reverse the increase in anthropogenic greenhouse gas emissions.

All we have to do now is to take these innovative and often brilliant pieces and combine them

FIGURE 3.2
We need the climate equivalent of fire halls to ensure climate protection in our daily lives.

into a comprehensive body of work that deals decisively with climate change.

Every time humanity was on the cusp of a decision where we had to choose whether to stay mired in the past or move forward to a brighter and better future, there were loud and strident voices that warned that it couldn't be done, was not feasible, or would be economically disastrous. The abolition of slavery, the abolition of child labour, the recognition of women's right to vote, and, more recently, the passage of environmental laws such as the ones banning lead from gasoline and banning ozone-layer-depleting chlorofluorocarbons under the Montreal Protocol are cases in point.

In another example, in 2002 Norway's then Minister of Trade and Industry, Ansgar Gabrielson, introduced a law that required publicly traded companies to include at least 40% female members on their boards. This regulation was based on evidence that companies with boards that had both male and female representation were more successful financially.[35, 36, 37, 38] Even though there was some strong opposition to the law initially, most objectors turned to supporters in short order as the success of the measure became evident in the marketplace.[39]

Gender Diversity Increases Profits

"The 25 Fortune 500 firms with the best record of promoting women to high positions are between 18 and 69 percent more profitable than the median Fortune 500 firms in their industries."

~ Roy D. Adler, Pepperdine University, 2002[36]

Eliminating greenhouse gas emissions not only will protect us from the potentially catastrophic consequences of severe climate change, but will also create stronger and more stable economies, healthier individuals, and more resilient municipalities. And, of course, taking action on climate change will ultimately ensure that there will still *be* an economy, period.

"You Want This by *When?*"

There were strong indications that climate change would be a very serious problem even before the IPCC First Assessment Report in 1990. What has humanity's collective response been in the intervening 18 years?

Through our actions, we have *increased* the rate at which carbon dioxide is added to the atmosphere from around 1.3 parts per million (ppm) in 1990 to 1.8 ppm in 2001 (ten-year averages, including five years before and after the respective dates). In other words, since humanity became aware of the problem, we have *accelerated* the rate at which we are adding carbon dioxide to the atmosphere, rather than reduced it.

Each year we delay actions to control emissions will add to the accumulating levels of greenhouse gases and will make our job that much harder. Worse yet, scientists are not agreed on the greenhouse gas level which may represent a "tipping point" at which climate change becomes an unstoppable positive (self-reinforcing) feedback loop.

Examples of potential positive feedback loops include the following:

- Increased absorption of sunlight in the Arctic due to the melting of ice (ice has a high "albedo" or reflectivity, which means that it reflects more solar radiation back to space than open ocean water)

- Release of methane from frozen Arctic Ocean methane hydrate reserves due to hydrate melting induced by rising ocean temperatures (methane is a greenhouse gas more than 20 times stronger than carbon dioxide), further adding to atmospheric greenhouse gas levels[40]

- Decomposition of formerly frozen organic matter in Arctic tundra soils resulting in the release of additional carbon dioxide, further fueling climate change[41]

- Increased release of carbon dioxide due to drought-induced forest fires.

Furthermore, oceans, which have been — and still are — acting as carbon sinks, have been absorbing a large part of the carbon dioxide added by humans to the atmosphere. However, in recent years the ocean absorption of carbon has halved, indicating that some portion of the sink no longer accepts our excess carbon. The question is at which point we could reach a "runaway" greenhouse effect. There is some indication that a rise in global temperatures by 2°C or more could represent such a tipping point.

NASA's top climate scientist, James Hansen, believes that CO_2 levels must be reduced from the current 385 ppm to at most 350 ppm for a stable climate, and that we have *less* than ten years to act. [42]

The IPCC Fourth Assessment does not predict irreversible climate change if strong action is not taken within a decade. Rather, the IPCC points out that we do not know if a runaway greenhouse effect exists, and, if so, at which greenhouse gas concentration.

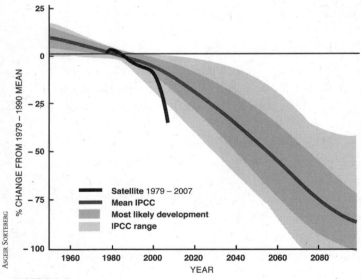

FIGURE 3.3
Satellite imaging shows that Arctic sea ice is melting more rapidly than the most pessimistic predictions of the Intergovernmental Panel on Climate Change (IPCC) projected. [43]

However, even the chair of the IPCC, Rajendra K. Pachauri has stated that some indicators of climate change, in particular the melting of Arctic ice, have progressed far more quickly than even the most pessimistic assumptions stated in the IPCC Fourth Assessment of December 2007 (Figure 3.3).

Even Shell Oil is adding its voice to those demanding significant action in less than a decade through its partnership in Principal Voices, principal voices.com. An increasing number of reasonable people insist that our window of opportunity may be ten years, or even less, maybe five years.

Meeting Al Gore's July 17, 2008 "generational challenge" of providing all of America's electricity needs through 100% renewable energy sources is a bold step, and we also have to meet the rest of our energy needs through efficiency and renewable sources, plus work on eliminating excess methane from the atmosphere.

QuickLink: CarbonCharter.org/04

The Ten-Year Target: 2018

This is our challenge, then: to move towards a zero-carbon society in ten years or less. This would require a 10% reduction in greenhouse gas emissions per year over the next decade.

In the worst case, this may save us from catastrophic climate change, and in the best case, it may prevent the suffering of hundreds of millions of people who would otherwise be displaced by changes in sea level, lose their homes from floods, or face food scarcity from droughts.

MORE INFO

• A discussion of the 350 ppm tipping point can be found in Michael D. Lemonick's September 2008 article "Beyond the

Tipping Point" in *Scientific American Earth 3.0*, available online at sciam.com/article.cfm?id=global-warming-beyond-the-co2.
- Websites addressing urgent action on climate change to prevent reaching a tipping point include 350.org and onehundred months.org.
- The International Code Council iccsafe.org has developed an International Energy Conservation Code iccsafe.org/ iccsafe.org/ that can serve as a blueprint for some of the aspects of a climate code.
- Information on the European Project for Equal Pay is at equal pay.nu/en_fakta.html.

ZERO-CARBON POLICIES

The following section describes some of the most breathtaking municipal, state, and federal initiatives to move towards a zero-carbon society. These initiatives from around the world demonstrate that there has been farsighted governance at many levels of government, with zero-carbon policies dating back more than a decade.[44]

Zero-Carbon Target Dates

UK: Zero-Carbon Homes

The UK is the world's first country to adopt a zero-carbon policy for new homes (effective 2016), though recently Wales has announced that it will adopt zero-carbon policies for new homes that will come into effect even earlier (by 2011). The British government has now also tabled amendments as part of the planning bill that will require any national planning policy statements to show how they will accelerate the shift to a low-carbon economy. The change will require local authorities to align planning with the new policy as well. The change is designed to speed approval of renewable energy developments that will power 1.5 million homes but are currently clogged in the planning system. [45]

Sweden: Freedom From Oil

Swedish prime minister Göran Persson has committed to eliminate Sweden's dependence on oil and other fossil fuels by 2020. Persson points out that Sweden has already cut its energy intensity by nearly 20% since 1994, through environmental taxes and by meeting 25% of energy needs through biofuel, at the same time experiencing higher per capita growth than the EU, the OECD, and the United States over the last ten years.[46]

Zero- and Low-Carbon Targets

A number of municipalities from around the world have committed to a 100% reduction in greenhouse gas emissions (see pp. 31, 32, 38, and 39). However, even non-zero-carbon targets are impressive. Germany is offering to achieve a reduction in greenhouse gas emissions of 40% below 1990 levels by 2020, provided the EU commits to a minimum 30% reduction and other nations target comparable reductions.[47]

Ashton Hayes

"The village of Ashton Hayes in Cheshire, England, is aiming to be the first carbon-neutral community in England. In just two years, the 1,000 residents have saved 20 percent on their energy costs and transformed their community (Figure 3.4).

'It's been great fun and an amazing boost in community spirit,' said Garry Charnock, who put the idea to some friends in the local pub. 'I thought they'd think of me as a bit of a crank, but they were all for it.'

More than 75 percent of the village showed up for the first meetings, something that had never happened before. Charnock told IPS that people are worried about climate change and want to do something but are reluctant to do it on their own.

Unwittingly, Charnock's notion of a carbon-neutral village unleashed the power of community."

~ Stephen Leahy, "Straightgoods.ca: Simple measures can cut carbon emissions."[48] See also Every ActionCounts.org.uk/en/fe/page.asp?n1=6&n2=120

Fossil-Fuel Free Växjö

In 1996, the Swedish city of Växjö decided to become fossil-fuel free. Växjö is located at 56° north, in the southern Swedish province of Småland. The municipality has a population of 78,000 and is home to over 7,000 companies.

With the vision to become "a city where it is easy and profitable to live a good life without fossil fuels," the city reduced its carbon dioxide emissions by 30% per capita by 2006, deriving more than half of its energy from renewables. This achievement is all the more remarkable since 39% of heating energy was already derived from renewable sources in 1993, due to the actions the city had taken in the '80s in response to the oil crisis. Per capita emissions in 2005 were 3.5 tonnes (7,700 pounds) of CO_2. Oil use decreased from 40% in 1993 to 15% in 2003. However, the use of energy for transporation has fallen more slowly in the municipality. While transport accounted for 49% of carbon emissions in 1993, it accounted for 79% in 2005 (Figure 3.5). Only since 2005 have transportation-related CO_2 emissions slowly begun to fall due to the use of more environmentally friendly cars and bio-fuels.[49, 50, 51, 52]

DENISE DAHL

FIGURE 3.4
Ashton Hayes is aiming to be England's first carbon-free community (image shows wind turbine on the roof of Ashton Hayes Primary School).

Fossil Carbon Dioxide Emissions per capita in Växjö (kg CO2)

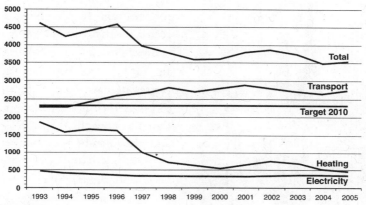

FIGURE 3.5
Carbon dioxide emissions from transportation, heating, and electricity in the municipality of Växjö in kg CO_2 per person and year, from 1993 to 2005, showing a 30% net reduction.

A new study program, Sustainable Energy Systems in Advanced Cities (SESAC), will cost € 9.7 million (US$14.6 million), € 3.9 million (US$5.8 million) of which the European Commission and the Swedish government are contributing. The program, with 19 partners from 6 European cities and coordinated by Växjö, will research district cooling systems, energy-efficient wooden house construction, biogas vehicle fuel, and demand-side management (Figure 3.6).[52]

> *"The City of Växjö hereby declares its aim that all energy shall come from renewable sources."*
>
> ~ Växjö, 1996

How Was It Accomplished?

Here is how the City of Växjö went about achieving its remarkable reductions in carbon emissions:

- The task force includes members of all political parties, representatives of industry and non-governmental organizations

COPYRIGHT DAVID BROBERG FLICKR.COM/PHOTOS/ DBROBERG/

FIGURE 3.6
The city of Växjö, recipient of the 2007 Baltic State award, bills itself as "The greenest city in Europe."

(NGOs), and citizens.

- The city is using more biomass for heating. In the heating sector, nearly 90% of energy comes from renewable sources.

- In the transportation sector, emissions have been reduced through the increased adoption of energy-efficient vehicles and the blending of biofuel (including ethanol) with gasoline and diesel, though net energy use did not start declining until 2005.

- Located in a forested area, the city emphasizes the use of forest products for energy as a bioregional approach, without diminishing biodiversity and while increasing forest cover.

- Small- and large-scale biomass-based district heating and cooling is used.

- The city also features energy-efficient street lighting, solar panels (municipal subsidies), cycle paths, and energy-efficient buildings.

- Electricity is derived from biomass (forest waste from within a 100 km/62 mile radius) and imports of renewable hydro- and wind power from outside the municipal jurisdiction.

- Cutting-edge building standards are mandatory for new construction, including submetering for apartments, mandatory hookups to the district heating system for new buildings, and the use of wooden construction to lower embodied energy costs.

- The city core has been converted to a pedestrian zone, with "car crossings" instead of pedestrian crossings. Free parking is provided for environmentally friendly cars and snow is regularly removed from bike paths as well as city streets.
- Biogas from sewage is used for electricity production.
- Mayor Bo Frank and the vice mayor assumed leadership and full responsibility for the project, giving it high status in the administration and the local community.
- The decision by city council to stop using fossil fuels for the activities of the municipality was unanimous.
- The biomass-to-energy chain, ecotourism, and technical site visits resulted in increased job creation.
- The city introduced a cycle campaign for municipal employees as well as access to a bicycle pool.
- Rather than solely looking at the direct dollar costs of city projects, the city uses ecoBUDGET, a model for environmental budgeting of natural resources, for their decision-making.[49, 51, 53]

The Decoupling of CO_2 Emissions and Economic Growth

Since 1993, Sweden in general and Växjö in particular have shown a strong decoupling of economic growth and CO_2 emissions. From 1993 to 2005, economic production in Växjö, as measured by gross regional product (GRP), greatly increased per capita, while CO_2 emissions fell by 30% (a severe wind storm briefly depressed GRP in 2005 due to forest losses). During the same period, GDP in Sweden rose to the same per capital level as Växjö while CO_2 emissions fell by 10% (Figure 3.7).[54, 55]

What Are the Next Targets?

Växjö's current goals include carbon emission reductions of 50% by 2010 and a minimum 70% reduction by 2025, compared to 1993 (note: Kyoto Protocol targets are based on the year 1990 instead, but Växjö only has data since 1993).

The city is also working on consumer-initiated load control (demand-side management), large-scale bio-DME (dimethyl ether) Fischer-Tropsch fuel production for vehicle use in conjunction with car maker Volvo (Figure 3.8), a 20% increase in bicycle traffic by 2015 compared to 2004, and an intermodal terminal for domestic freight to promote transportation by railway.[52, 56, 57]

The city is even offering three- to four-day training courses with certification for city councillors, civil servants, and others in a variety of fields, including "climate thinking," "bioenergy," "energy efficiency," and "renewable energy production."

Zero Carbon?

It is interesting to note that since carbon dioxide emissions from heating and electricity generation have been virtually eliminated in Växjö (about 0.7 tonnes/ 1,650 pounds per capita remaining), transportation now accounts for fully 79% of all carbon dioxide emissions (Figure 3.5). Through adoption of plug-in hybrid tech-

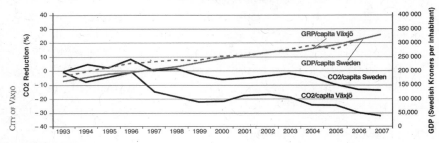

FIGURE 3.7
Carbon emission reductions vs. economic growth for Sweden and the Swedish municipality of Växjö, showing a decoupling of the two factors.

nology proven on roads today, coupled with biofuel conversions, it is not much of a leap at all to envision a decarbonization to a zero-carbon economy for Växjö, today.

VOLVO BUS INC.

FIGURE 3.8
Växjö is working towards fueling municipal buses with DME biofuel.

Awards

In 2000 the City of Växjö received a prestigious international environmental prize from the International Council for Local Environmental Initiatives (ICLEI) (iclei.org), an international association of local governments for sustainability, and in 2007 it received the Sustainable Energy Europe Award of the European Commission.[50, 53]

MORE INFO

• Växjö website: vaxjo.se
• Summary of new Växjö initiatives from the 2007 Climate Summit in New York City: nycclimatesummit.com/casestudies/energy/energy_vaxjo.html

RESOURCES

• Fossil Fuel Free Växjö: vaxjo.se/upload/3880/CO2%20engelska%202007.pdf
• Certification courses for city councillors and civil servants: vaxjo.se/upload/19330/Technical%20visits%20menu.pdf
  QuickLink: CarbonCharter.org/05

Woodstock: Zero Carbon by 2017

On March 13, 2007, the Town of Woodstock, New York, located 70 km/43 miles from the site of the eponymous legendary concert held in 1969, passed a resolution to become the first zero-carbon municipality in the US. Towards this goal, the community has completed a number of initiatives:

- installation of 112 photovoltaic (solar electric) modules on the town hall, with a capacity of 16.8 kilowatts, allowing it to feed excess electricity into the grid
- subsidies for wind power installations
- the installation of a geothermal heating-cooling system at the town garage
- a tree-planting program to increase summer shading

Planned initiatives include:

- steps to increase the fuel efficiency of town vehicles and a program to offer anti-idling education for town employees
- bylaws to ensure that buildings conform to the standards of the Energy Star and US Green Building Council rating systems
- the promotion of renewable energy resources
- the establishment of a global warming task force
- the adoption of a land-use policy that reduces sprawl and creates walkable communities that preserve open space
- steps to increase the efficiency of the pumps for the town's water and sewage systems and to recover methane from wastewater treatment for energy production
- a motion for raising bonds of up to US$1.45 million to rehabilitate the town hall (which also houses the court, the police department, and emergency services), including upgrades to the building's energy efficiency

MORE INFO

Low- and zero-carbon policies

- The Maldives are the first country to announce their commitment to go carbon neutral within 10 years:
  news.bbc.co.uk/2/hi/science/nature/7944760.stm
- Other countries committing to zero-carbon goals include Norway, Iceland, New Zealand and Monaco:
  timesofindia.indiatimes.com/Health—Science/Earth/Global-Warming/Maldives-plans-to-become-first-carbon-neutral-nation/articleshow/4264462.cms
- The number of municipalities having signed on to British Columbia's "Climate Action Charter" (carbon neutral with respect to their operations by 2012) has now risen to more than 130:
  cd.gov.bc.ca/ministry/docs/climate_action_charter.pdf
- On March 17, 2009, Copenhagen announced that it is the world's first capital city committing to becoming carbon neutral. Copenhagen aims to achieve this within 16 years (i.e. by 2025):
  c40cities.org/news/news-20090317.jsp
- Masdar, the world's first zero carbon city is being built near Abu Dhabi, United Arab Emirates: en.wikipedia.org/wiki/Masdar_City

QuickLink: CarbonCharter.org/06

OTHER CARBON POLICIES

Carbon Footprint Product Labels

We are all familiar with food labels that contain ingredient lists and nutritional values, labels on clothes, and consumption ratings on appliances. Now, carbon labeling is making its appearance to help buyers make informed choices.

The UK government created and funded the independent company Carbon Trust in 2001 to help businesses reduce their carbon footprint. Working with the Carbon Trust and businesses since 2004, the UK Environment Ministry introduced a carbon label in

tonnes (2 million pounds) of CO_2 emissions and £1.2 million (about US$2.4 million) per year (Figures 3.9, 3.10).

Other companies that have adopted the labeling include the pharmacy chain Boots for their Botanics shampoo range, Innocent Smoothie, and supermarket chain Tesco for 20 products including laundry detergents, orange juice, light bulbs, and potatoes.

Coca-Cola, Cadbury-Schweppes, Kimberly Clark, and Muller Dairy (UK) have all committed to trialling the program.[62]

The Soil Association, the UK's largest certifier of organic food, pointed out that the current carbon label does not take into account the carbon storage results of farming methods. Long-term trials have shown that, compared to non-organic farming, organic farming adds between 0.4 and 1.5 tonnes of CO_2e (carbon dioxide equivalents) to the soil per hectare and year (300 to 1,300 pounds per acre). And even though organic products already come out well on carbon labels, including the carbon storage factor reduces the total greenhouse gas emissions of the organic foods examined by 25 to 75% compared to non-organic food, all other things being equal.[68]

Other Jurisdictions

Japan's Ministry of Economy, Trade and Industry established the Domestic Committee for International Standardization of the Carbon Footprint System in 2008 to bring together government, academics, industry, consumers, and certification groups to create a suitable carbon footprint system in Japan that integrates well with international ISO standards.[69]

Sapporo breweries in Japan is the first to provide carbon labels for its beer. One 350 ml (12 fluid ounces) can of beer was found to create about 590 grams (1.3 pounds) of CO_2e.[70, 71]

In Germany, the Öko-Institut (Institue for Applied Ecology), the Potsdam Institute for Climate Impact Research, and market research firms are piloting a Product Carbon Footprint system in collaboration with leading companies. One goal of the German research is to find a system that is harmonized with global standards so that it can be effective for internationally traded goods and services. Another initiative is a climate-neutral label; once products have been reduced by the maximum reasonable amount, the remainder may be offset by mitigating measures (external offsets). Meanwhile, the German government has announced that it will introduce a CO_2 labeling system for cars. The German postal service, Deutsche Post, is in the process of inventorying its greenhouse gas emissions and aims to make its letter delivery business climate-neutral.

The European Commission is examining whether the EU's Eco-label system can be extended to include carbon footprint information.[72]
   QuickLink: CarbonCharter.org/07

RESOURCES

• Website of the UK Carbon Trust, one of the principal proponents of carbon footprint product labels: carbon-label.co.uk
• Details of the UK PAS 2050 standard for carbon labels: BSIGroup.com

US Mayors Climate Protection Agreement

In the absence of any US federal commitments to reduce greenhouse gas emissions, on February 16, 2005, the day the Kyoto Protocol came into force, Seattle Mayor Greg Nickels launched the US Mayors Climate Protection Agreement (Figure 3.11).[73] Since 2007, the Agreement has been tracked by the United States Conference of Mayors. The members of the Conference consist of American cities with a population of 30,000 or more, including 1,139 such cities in 2007.[74] By October, 2008, 884 mayors of the 1,139 cities of the US Conference of Mayors had signed on to the program.[75]

Under the agreement, participating cities commit to take the following three actions:

• strive to meet or beat the Kyoto Protocol targets in their own communities, through actions ranging from anti-sprawl

COURTESY SEATTLE MUNICIPAL ARCHIVES

FIGURE 3.11
Seattle Mayor Greg Nickels launched the US Mayors Climate Protection Agreement in 2005.

land-use policies to urban forest restoration projects to public information campaigns;

- urge both their state governments and the federal government to enact policies and programs to meet or beat the greenhouse gas emission reduction target suggested for the United States in the Kyoto Protocol (7% reduction from 1990 levels by 2012); and

- urge the US Congress to pass the bipartisan greenhouse gas reduction legislation, which would establish a national emissions trading system.[76]

Other Jurisdictions

On January 29, 2008, the European Commission launched the European Covenant of Mayors. Signing cities formally commit to efforts beyond those of the EU commitments, namely a unilateral minimum 20% reduction in CO_2 emissions by 2020. Within two months of the announcement, 141 cities had expressed their intention to sign the Covenant by January 15, 2009.[77]

RESOURCES

- Mayors Climate Protection Center: usmayors.org/climate protection/
- Best practice examples from municipalities throughout the US: usmayors.org/climateprotection/documents/2007bestpractices-mcps.pdf
- To download the US Mayors Climate Protection Agreement: usmayors.org/climateprotection/MayorsClimateAgreementSig naturePage.pdf

- Link to the European Covenant of Mayors: sustenergy.org/tpl/page.cfm?pageName=covenant_of_mayors2
QuickLink: CarbonCharter.org/08

Carbon Accounting and Green Accounting

The gross national product (GNP) as a measure of a nation's welfare has been criticized on two counts: Is the GNP truly the measure of a nation's welfare, and does it adequately take into account a nation's natural capital?

Nordhaus and Tobin, two Yale economists, argued in 1973 that a market system that does not ascribe a value to, for example, clean air, provides an unreasonable subsidy to polluting cars and polluting forms of electricity production whereas in an economy in which polluters pay, there are market incentives for the development of low-pollution processes. (However, Nordhaus and Tobin also pointed out that potential global environmental catastrophes, such as climate change, cannot necessarily be addressed by economic systems alone).[78]

Green Accounting 1

"What gets measured, gets managed."

~ Anonymous

Green or environmental accounting includes natural capital in its balance sheet (Figure 3.12). China, the Netherlands, and the Philippines have all implemented components of green accounting, but no regular reporting yet, according to economist Gernot Wagner.[79, 80] The UK introduced environmental accounting in 2002.

In 1995, the US Congress inexplicably suspended efforts by the Bureau of Economic Analysis to include natural resources in GDP. The National Research Council's Committee on National Statistics conducted an independent review that provides a clear mandate for green accounting and was released in 1999 under the title *Nature's Numbers: Expanding the National Economic Accounts to Include the Environment*[81], a summary of which can be found at rff.org/rff/Documents/RFF-Resources-139-greengdp.pdf. The

National Academy of Sciences has also endorsed the concept of green accounting.[82]

Green Accounting 2

"What gets measured, gets treasured."

~ Anonymous

Adding accounting for the global carbon commons would be an important component of green accounting and has the added advantage of being a factor that is relatively easily quantified.

Numerous cities around the world have started to track the emissions of their greenhouse gases, including carbon dioxide.

"Sustainable development ... refers at once to economic, social and environmental needs."

~ United Nations, European Commission, International Monetary Fund, Organisation for Economic Co-operation and Development, and World Bank, "Handbook of National Accounting: Integrated Environmental and Economic Accounting 2003"[83]

Examples and Case Studies: United Kingdom

The United Kingdom has kept environmental accounts since 2002, tracking factors such as natural capital (oil and gas reserves, land cover, forestry, and fish stocks), physical flows (including energy consumption), atmospheric emissions (including greenhouse gases), material flows, waste and water, and environmental taxes and protection expenditures.[84]

CHRISTIAN MIHAI VELA – STOCKEXPERT

FIGURE 3.12
Green accounting moves natural capital into a quantifiable and trackable sphere.

MORE INFO

• For the United Kingdom environmental accounting

reports see statistics.gov.uk/statbase/Product.asp?vlnk=3698.
- The United Nations Environment Programme has a website providing tools and resources for green accounting at unep.ch/etb/areas/VRC_index.php.
- A rationale for green accounting is provided by Gernot Wagner, a Harvard and Stanford trained economist working for the Environmental Defense Fund at gwagner.com/writing/2004/04/fixing-gdp-green-accounting-in-united.html.
- More general information on green accounting can be found at copperwiki.org/index.php/Green_Accounting.
- An evaluation of Australia's national carbon accounting system can be downloaded from climatechange.gov.au/ncas/reports/pubs/ncasevalfinal.pdf.

QuickLink: CarbonCharter.org/09

Genuine Progress Indicators

In 1995, the non-profit organization Redefining Progress rprogress.org introduced the concept of the "Genuine Progress Indicator" (GPI). The GPI starts out with GDP, but adds indicators that are not measured in a market economy, such as housework, volunteering, higher education, increased leisure time, and a longer lifespan of consumer products on the positive side of the balance sheet, and items such as crime, pollution, defense expenditures, and inequality in wealth distribution on the negative side.[85] According to Wikipedia, at least 11 countries, including Austria, England, Sweden, and Germany have recalculated their GDP using the Genuine Progress Indicator.[86]

In a related approach, in 1972, Bhutan's King Jigme Singye Wangchuk coined the term "Gross National Happiness" (GNH) in response to criticism that his country's GNP was not growing much. Bhutan has adopted an official policy in which GNH takes precedence over GNP, placing the well-being and happiness of its citizens above material consumption.

MORE INFO

- Redefining Progress' site on the Genuine Progress Indicator: rprogress.org/sustainability_indicators/genuine_progress_indicator.htm
- Wikipedia on the Genuine Progress Indicator: en.wikipedia.org/wiki/Genuine_Progress_Indicator
- On Bhutan's Gross National Happiness: Mark Anielski. 2007. *The Economics of Happiness: Building Genuine Wealth*. New Society Publishers.
  QuickLink: CarbonCharter.org/10

Genuine Wealth Indices

Edmonton ecological economist Mark Anielski has refined the Genuine Progress Indicator as a local instrument for measuring genuine wealth through a process that determines criteria that are relevant for local communities. These criteria can vary from community to community, but they are the ultimate measures of the factors that are locally considered indicators of wealth and happiness. These factors can then be tracked and measured to determine whether the community is succeeding in increasing or decreasing the composite of the factors.

Examples and Case Studies: City of Leduc, Alberta

In 2005, the City of Leduc, in cooperation with the Leduc-Nisku region in Alberta, Canada, decided to initiate an innovative Genuine Wealth Project for their region. The study did not merely compare gross domestic product (GDP) with neighboring communities, but addressed a comprehensive list of indicators of quality of life.

The first step of the project was a survey of citizens to determine which key wealth indicators are considered of importance to the community. The second step was to quantify identified parameters, including self-rated happiness, life expectancy, infant mortality, deaths due to cancer and heart disease, asthma and suicide rates, physical activity, employment rates, educational attainment, average class sizes and library access, ethnic diversity, trust and belonging, safety, crime, equity and fairness, community vitality, voter turnout, GDP, median total income, food bank use, access to stores and services, dependence on government safety nets, access to affordable housing, municipal tax rates, transportation, recreation, and other public infrastructure, biking and walking trails, public transit, ecological footprint, availability of prime agricultural land, green space, forest cover, water and air quality, greenhouse gas emissions, water use and storage capacity, waste production and recycling, residential energy use, renewable energy, and numerous other features.

The third step involved benchmarking the data against the past performance of the municipality as well as regional comparisons to neighboring municipalities or state/provincial levels. (As this was the first study, only a regional comparison was possible.) The

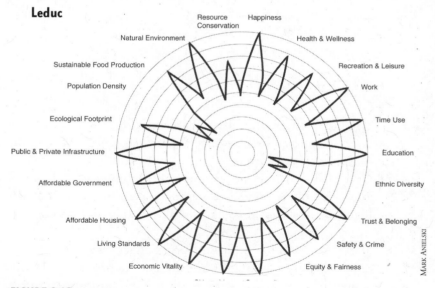

FIGURE 3.13
The composite sustainability of genuine wealth assesses a community's vitality and happiness level.[87]

CITY OF LEDUC

FIGURE 3.14
Leduc, Alberta, Canada, in cooperation with the Leduc-Nisku Region, was one of the first municipalities to undertake a study of the indicators of its genuine wealth.

resulting information provided the first comprehensive overview of the state of the community and areas in which the municipal region excelled or lagged behind, yielding a composite value that exceeded the regional index of Genuine Wealth by nearly 10% (Figures 3.13, 3.14).[88]

MORE INFO

- For information on the Leduc-Nisku Region 2005 Genuine Wealth Project, visit city.leduc.ab.ca/Leduc/.
- For other examples of Genuine Wealth and ecological footprint studies, see anielski.com.
- General information on carbon policies, using Canada as an example, can be found at Choosing Greenhouse Gas Emission Reduction Policies in Canada, available at pubs.pembina.org/reports/pembina-td-final.pdf.
- North America's first regional (and revenue neutral) carbon tax came into force July 1, 2008 in the Canadian province of British Columbia: gov.bc.ca/fortherecord/carbon/cr_taxpayers.html?src=/ taxpayers/cr_taxpayers.html
  QuickLink: CarbonCharter.org/11

ENERGY EFFICIENCY

"The US's electric bill could be halved through energy-efficiency measures and renewables that would mostly pay for themselves in a year. That's not a free lunch. It's a lunch you're paid to eat."

- Amory Lovins[89]

WHOLE BOOKS CAN BE FILLED WITH THE TECHNOLOGIES, POLICIES, and incentives that can vastly increase the energy efficiency of our cities, homes, and industry. For decades, Hunter and Amory Lovins have been among those who have argued convincingly that energy efficiency is our number one green source of energy. (Their respective current organizations are the Rocky Mountain Institute rmi.org and Natural Capitalism Solutions natcapsolutions.org.) "Negawatt" is the term they have used to describe a watt of energy that is no longer being consumed due to the implementation of energy efficiency measures.

These two publications provide excellent starting points for examining the potential of energy efficiency (Figure 4.1):

- Paul Hawken, Amory Lovins, and L. Hunter Lovins. 1999. *Natural Capitalism*. Little, Brown and Company.

- Amory B. Lovins, E. Kyle Datta, Odd-Even Bustnes, Jonathan G. Koomey, and Nathan J. Glasgow. 2004. Winning the Oil Endgame: Innovation for Profits, Jobs and Security. Rocky Mountain Institute. Available for free (with registration) at oilendgame.com.

    QuickLink: CarbonCharter.org/12

The following sections present a few examples of energy efficiency initiatives.

ENERGY LABELING FOR HOMES

Energy Performance Certificate

The energy performance certificate is a document created by a third party that states a building's rated energy consumption based on standardized calculation criteria. It gives renters or purchasers of buildings a reliable tool for estimating their future utility costs and allows direct comparisons of the environmental desirability of different buildings.

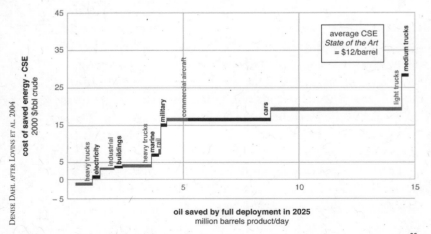

4.1 Potential carbon reductions to be realized from increased gains in energy efficiency.[90]

Purpose and Benefits

The energy performance certificate (EPC) and other home energy labeling systems are government-mandated ratings that state a building's energy consumption based on standardized calculation criteria. It gives renters or purchasers of buildings a reliable tool for estimating their future utility costs and allows direct comparisons of the environmental desirability of different buildings.

An EPC provides a powerful incentive for builders and property owners to create buildings that are energy-efficient and to retrofit existing buildings. Property owners have a greater incentive to provide energy-efficient buildings when they know that better designs will allow them to rent or sell their properties more quickly or for higher rates. EPCs create a market for efficient buildings by ensuring that investments in energy efficiency are rewarded in the marketplace.

An EPC also gives purchasers or renters a powerful tool for selecting a building that has low utility costs and less of an environmental impact.

Examples and Case Studies: The UK Energy Performance Certificate (EPC)

Since April 2006, all new homes in the UK required an interim energy assessment. However, since October 2008, all buildings in the UK that are constructed, sold or rented out require the full Energy Performance Certificate in accordance with the European Energy Performance of Buildings Directive initiated in 2002 (Figures 4.2, 4.3, 4.4).[93, 94, 95, 96] The EPC is also part of the mandatory Home Condition Report that has to be provided free of charge to any prospective buyer; it includes information on the age of the building, the exterior and interior condition of the house, services, easements, and serious defects.[97] While the energy assessment was initially required only for homes, the EPC now also applies to businesses. The EPC is valid for three years (up from the initial one year period). Costs for EPCs range from £35 to

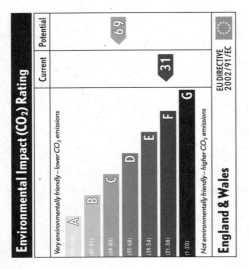

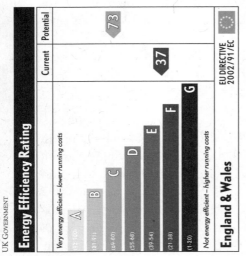

UK Government

FIGURE 4.2
The UK Energy Performance Certificate required for all new buildings and all buildings bought or sold since October 2008. According to the universal European energy rating system, the letter "A" stands for the best rating, while "G" is worst.[91]

£300, depending on the type of assessment.

One of the features of the EPC is that it lists measures the building owner can undertake to cut carbon emissions and energy bills (recommendations list estimated costs as "low" or "high," but give no exact cost quotes).[98]

It is thought that the EPC may be used for an "energy taxation" in the future, whereby poorly rated buildings are subject to higher taxes.[99] (Germany uses a similar scheme for cars, where cars with a higher engine capacity require higher annual car registration fees). New UK buildings with a zero-carbon footprint are already relieved of "stamp duty" (property tax) until 2012 (see page 30, *UK: Zero-Carbon Homes*).[100]

Furthermore, since 2008, larger (over 10,000 m²/ 110,000 sq. ft.) public buildings in the UK must show a Display Energy Certificate (DEC) to allow the public to see how efficient each building

EPBD implementation date for legal requirement of energy performance certification for buildings sold or rented.

	NEW HOMES	EXISTING HOMES	NEW COMMERCIAL	EXISTING COMMERCIAL	NEW PUBLIC	EXISTING PUBLIC
Austria	2008	2009	2008	2009	2008	2009
Belgium	*2008	*2009	*2008	*2009	*2008	*2009
Bulgaria					2005	2005
Cyprus	*2009	*2009	*2009	*2009	*2009	*2009
Croatia						
Czech Republic	2009		2009		2009	2009
Denmark	2006	2006	2006	2006	2006	2006
Estonia	2009	2009	2009	2009	2009	2009
France	2007	2006	2007	2006	2007	2008
Finland	2008		2008	2009	2008	
Germany	2002	2009	2002	2009	2002	2009
Greece	2009	2009	2009	2009	2009	2009
Hungary						
Ireland	2007	2009	2008	2009	2008	2009
Italy	2009	2009	2008	2008	2007	2007
Latvia						
Lithuania	2007	2009	2007	2009	2007	2009
Luxembourg	2007	2007	2007	2007	2007	
Malta	*2009	*2009	*2009	*2009	*2009	*2009
Netherlands	2008	2008	2008	2008	*2009	*2009
Norway						
Poland	2008	2009	2008	2009	2008	2009
Portugal	2007	2009	2007	2009	2007	2008
Romania	2007	2010	2007	2010	2007	2007
Slovak Republic	2008	2008	2008	2008	2008	2008
Slovenia	*2008	*2009	*2008	*2009	*2008	*2008
Spain	2007	*2009	2007	*2009	2007	*2009
Sweden	2009	2009	2009	2009	2008	2008
United Kingdom	2008	2008	2008	2008	2008	2008

* expected date

FIGURE 4.3
Introduction dates for Energy Performance Certificates (EPCs) in European Union member states.[92]

is. The DEC has to be accompanied by an Advisory Report that lists cost-effective measures to improve the building's energy rating. The government is considering extending this system to private-sector buildings.[94]

UK GOVERNMENT

FIGURE 4.4
Poster promoting the UK's Energy Performance Certificate, mandatory in the UK since 2008.

Other Jurisdictions

Austria implemented mandatory EPCs for the buying and selling of new buildings in 2008 and of existing buildings in 2009. The same or similar dates apply to Belgium. In Germany, certification requirements already became law in 2002.[92] For other dates of European Community implementation, see Figure 4.3.

Canada has a government-developed EnerGuide system that is used to determine eligibility for government grants. R-2000 is a voluntary standard of energy efficiency under which over 14,000 homes have been built in Canada and which improves the thermal performance of buildings by 30%.[100] In the US, EnergyStar

"We can claim tax credits for living in zero-carbon homes."

GRIZELDA

rated buildings have improved performance over standard buildings. However, the required improvement is only 15%.[101] Furthermore, on the federal level neither of these programs is mandated, either for existing or new buildings.

MORE INFO

- 2002 European Performance of Buildings Directive (EPBD): eur-lex.europa.eu/LexUriServ/LexUriServ.do?uri=OJ:L:2003:001:0065:0071:EN:PDF
- 2006 EPBD Certification FAQ and update: buildingsplatform.org/cms/index.php?id=93
- 2008 Display Energy Certificates (DECs) for public buildings in the UK: communities.gov.uk/planningandbuilding/theenvironment/energyperformance/publications/displayenergycertificates
- Review of the implementation of the Energy Performance Certification in 27 member states: buildingsplatform.eu/ epbd_publication/doc/EPBD_BuPLa_Country%20reports_20080624_2_p3126.pdf

QuickLink: CarbonCharter.org/13

CLL-SOHRABJI GODREJ GREEN BUSINESS CENTRE

FIGURE 4.5
The LEED® rating system of Green Building Councils from around the world certifies build-ings based on their sustainability features (photo shows the world's first LEED® 2.0 Platinum building, the Confederation of Indian Industry's Sohrabji Godrej Green Business Centre in Hyderabad, India).

Jurisdictions requiring LEED certification for their buildings

RICHARD KRAUSE, GODO STOYKE

Name	Jurisdiction type	Location	Country	LEED level required	Scope
Alameda	City	CA	USA	Certified	All city-owned and city-funded projects exceeding $3 million in construction costs
Alameda	County	CA	USA	Silver	All county projects
Albany	City	CA	USA	Certified	All city sponsored construction projects of at least 5,000 square feet of occupied nonresidential space
Albany	City	CA	USA	Certified	Private commercial projects at 10,000 sq. ft.
Albuquerque	City	NM	USA	Silver	All city-owned and city-funded projects 5,000 sq. ft. or more and/or using over 50 KW electrical demand
Anaheim	City	CA	USA	Certified	All city-owned projects larger than 10,000 square feet
Annapolis	City	MD	USA	Silver	All public construction
Annapolis	City	MD	USA	Certified	New commercial and mixed-use buildings of 7,500 sq. ft. or greater
Arlington	Town	MA	USA	Silver	All new buildings and renovation projects
Asheville	City	NC	USA	Gold	All new, occupied, city-owned buildings greater than or equal to 5,000 sq. ft.

FIGURE 4.6
Jurisdictions in Canada and the US requiring LEED® certification for new buildings (LEED® is the Leadership in Energy and Environmental Design certification of the US and Canada Green Building Councils). Sample listing – see QuickLink for the complete listing.

BUILDING CODES

LEED Standards

An increasing number of municipalities, states, and provinces require all new buildings to be certified to LEED® (Leadership in Energy and Environmental Design) standards, the rating system of the United States and Canada Green Building Councils (usgbc.org and cagbc.org) (Figure 4.5).

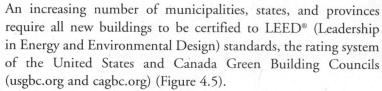

LEED® includes a set of mandatory requirements that must be fulfilled for any LEED® certification as well as a comprehensive catalog of optional measures within the framework of a points system that determines whether an application gets a certified, silver, gold or platinum LEED® rating. Figure 4.6 lists jurisdictions that have adopted mandatory LEED® certification for new government buildings. A number of municipalities have even begun to make LEED® certification a requirement for commercial building permits.

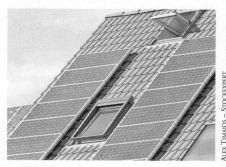

FIGURE 4.7
Solar access bylaws are key in ensuring that passive and active solar systems and absorption chilling can operate at maximum efficiency in sustainable buildings.

For US municipal green building code initiatives accessible by state, see iccsafe. org/news/ green/map.html.

QuickLink: CarbonCharter.org/14

QuickLink: See CarbonCharter.org/15 for the complete listing.

Solar Access

Solar access is critical for hot water solar collectors, for photovoltaic (solar electric) cells, and even for passive solar gain for buildings. Especially between 10 am and 2 pm, when the sun is at its highest elevation, solar access needs to be unobstructed for significant solar gain (Figures 4.7, 4.8).

Municipalities are beginning to incorporate solar access into their code; for example, the City of Bend, Oregon, introduced a number of sections that help building owners to obtain solar gain.

Solar Access: The City of Bend, Oregon

The Bend Code contains two innovative sections for ensuring unfettered access to sunlight for passive solar gain and operation of solar cells and collectors, specified in "Solar Setbacks" (10-10.26A) and "Solar Access" (10-10.26B).

Solar Setbacks

Solar Setbacks

"The purpose of this section is to provide as much solar access as feasible during the winter solar heating hours to existing or potential buildings by requiring all new structures to be constructed as far south on their lots as is feasible and necessary."

~ Code 10-10.26A of the City of Bend, Oregon

The code contains a provision for solar setbacks that requires all new structures to be constructed as far south on their lots as feasible. The central business zone is exempt from the provision.[103]

Solar Access Permit

The Solar Access Permit section of the Bend code is intended to ensure that productive solar collectors are not shaded by neighboring vegetation. Removal of neighboring vegetation can only be applied for if no suitable alternate collector site can be found on the applicant's

Congress

"So maybe it is feel-good legislation — What's wrong with feeling good?"

lot. Cost of trimming is borne by the applicant if the vegetation existed at the time of permit application, and borne equally by the applicant and the neighbor for all other vegetation. [104]

Other Jurisdictions

California has introduced a number of acts promoting building owners' access to solar insolation, including, for example, the Solar Rights Act amended by AB 2473 that came into effect on January 1, 2005. This act states that "local agencies not adopt ordinances that create unreasonable barriers to the installation of solar energy systems, including, but not limited to, design review for aesthetic purposes."[105]

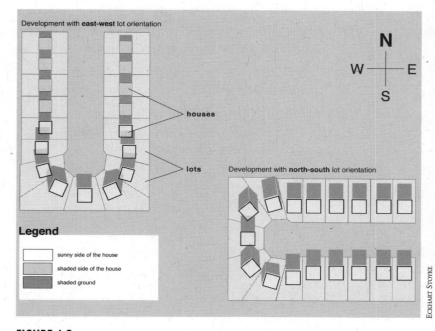

FIGURE 4.8
The simple introduction of an east-west orientation for roads by city planners in area structure plans can result in lowered heating bills of 5 to 60%.[102]

MORE INFO

- The Bend code is available at ci.bend.or.us/depts/community_development/planning_division.
- A summary of California State solar access laws can be found at solardepot.com/pdf/CASolarAccessLaws.pdf.
- A very comprehensive listing of US municipal, state, and federal solar and green incentives and programs is available at dsireusa.org.
- A Canadian listing of federal and provincial incentive programs can be found at cansia.ca/Default.aspx?pageId=139888.
QuickLink: CarbonCharter.org/16

Energy Star and LEED in US Federal Buildings

"In 2002, the U.S. Office of Management and Budget's Circular A-11 encouraged federal agencies to incorporate Energy Star ... or LEED into all designs for new buildings and renovations. As a result, many federal agencies or departments began to use LEED and most new federal buildings and renovations since that time have been LEED certified."

~ 2007 White Paper on Green Buildings
by the International Code Council[106]

TRANSPORTATION

WALKABLE AND RIDEABLE CITIES

Post-Carbon Cities: Transportation

"Deal with transportation and land use (or you may as well stop now). Fundamentally rethink your municipality's land use and transportation practices, from building and zoning codes to long-range planning. Make land use and transportation planning decisions with 100-year timeframes. Organize with neighboring jurisdictions to address the land use and transportation challenges of energy and climate uncertainty at a regional level."

~ Daniel Lerch, *Post Carbon Cities: Planning for Energy and Climate Uncertainty* [107]

Walkable Cities

WALKABLE COMMUNITIES INC., WALKABLE.ORG, A US non-profit corporation, is one of North America's foremost authorities on creating walkable communities (Figure 5.1).

DA BURDEN, GLATTING JACKSON KERCHER ANGLIN, INC.

FIGURE 5.1
A "walking audit" with Dan Burden of NGO Walkable Communities can reveal strengths and weaknesses of a municipality from a pedestrian's perspective.

The organization has identified 12 characteristics that greatly enhance a community's likelihood to enjoy heavy pedestrian traffic:

- Intact town centers. This includes a quiet and pleasant main street, a variety of personal services, including hairdressers, restaurants and delis, a post office, and services for youth and seniors, all within a quarter-mile (400 m) radius. For smaller cities and towns, this would likely also contain the city hall and library.

- Mixed-income, mixed-use neighborhoods. They allow residents to work where they live.

- Public spaces. Ideal public spaces — spaces that are accessible for everyone, where people can assemble and play — are located within one eighth of a mile (200 m) from neighborhoods.

- Universal design. Walkable communities feature ramps for universal access, benches, shade, and other designs that make walking enjoyable.

- Controlled speed for key streets. Tree-lined streets with on-street parking reduce traffic speeds to a safe and pleasant level.

- Linkage of streets and trails. Cul-de-sacs feature trail linkages to repair fractured patterns.

- Access to basic services within a 1/8- to a 1/2-mile radius. Distance to most services, including elementary schools, is 1/4 mile (400 m) or less. Parks are within 1/8 mile (200 m), high frequency buses within 1/4 to 1/2 mile (400 to 800 m), and high schools within 1 mile (1.6 km).

- Municipal design for people. Investments in public plazas, parks, and walkways are a sure sign of design for people. A review of building permits by category can reveal if construction is primarily diverse infill or single price-range housing.

- Think small. The most walkable towns are imposing maximum parking requirements rather than minimums. The City of Palo Alto limits grocery stores to 20,000 sq. ft. (just under 2,000 m2) to allow for more distributed grocery stores that remain competitive, yet can be largely reached on foot.

"Cars are happiest when there are no other cars around. People are happiest when there are other people around."

~ Dan Burden, walkable-city specialist, walkable.org

SUE ANNA JOE – STOCKXCHNG IMAGE

- Diversity of walkers. Some areas may seem walkable, but have few actual walkers. What are the reasons? Is it crime, lack of interesting destinations, limited hours of access? Good walkable communities are characterized by a diversity of walkers and bikers, young and old, those with disabilities and without, and often even courteous drivers!

- Municipal vision. Walkable Communities describes Seattle, Washington; Portland, Oregon; and Austin, Texas, as three municipalities that have developed neighborhood master plans. Honolulu budgets about US$1 million per year for each neighborhood.

- Visionary leaders. A majority of civic leaders aiming to create pleasant places for people to live and a champion on town council, the chamber of commerce, or the planning board are frequent hallmarks of walkable cities. [108]

Walkable Communities in Palo Alto

"Walkable communities are fine-grained, deeply rooted, diverse places where humans and our natural environment co-exist in a complex harmony and balance."

~ Yoriko Kashimoto, Mayor of
City of Palo Alto[109]

MORE INFO
- The website of Walkable Communities can be found at walkable.org.
QuickLink: CarbonCharter.org/17

Bikeable Cities

In 2008, an Austrian scientist by the name of Michael Meschik released a study in which he compares the bicycle grid of Holland to that of Austria. Austrians in the city of Linz complete about 5.4% of all trips on bicycle (compared to about 20% on public transit, 25% on foot, and nearly 50% by car). In contrast, the Dutch city of Amsterdam has a 400% higher adoption of bicycles as a means of transportion, with 27% of all trips being completed by bike.

At times of increasing fuel costs, why do many countries still have low levels of bike ridership? Meschik examined barriers to and incentives for bike riding in each country and came to a number of interesting and surprising conclusions.

Money

The Austrian city of Linz invests € 4.31 (about US$ 6.50) per citizen per year in bicycle infrastructure whereas the Dutch city of Amsterdam invests € 27 (about US$ 40) per person annually, more than six times as much.

Safe Bike Paths

The proper design of bike paths is key. Bike paths separated from roads by parked cars and trees may feel safer on a subjective level, but reduce visibility at intersections, leading to disproportionately higher numbers of accidents. An ideal bike path is immediately adjacent to the road and slightly elevated. Designing its bike paths in this way, the Danish capital, Copenhagen, reduced its bicycle-involved accident rate in spite of rising ridership — and the Austrian bicycle-Mecca of Salzburg (20% ridership) is now converting hidden bike paths back to road-integrated ones.

SANJA GJENERO – STOCKXCHNG IMAGE

Bicycle Security

Few things are more annoying than not finding one's bike where it had been parked because it was stolen. "Bike&Ride" secure bicycle facilities close to public transit stations have especially good potential to increase total ridership and are surprisingly cost-effective. Whereas a single parking stall for cars may cost between US$15,000 and US$45,000, costs for secure bike stalls are negligible (secure bike stalls may include guarded sites, lockable lockers, or stands with coded racks).

The ability to easily transport bikes on public transit, opening all one-way streets to bike traffic, equality for bicycles and cars in traffic bylaws, and bicycle traffic masterplans for larger cities have also been found to be effective in promoting the switch to bike-powered transportation.

Head Space

Role models are critical. City councillors who praise bicycle traffic but only hop onto a bike for a quick PR shot are counter-productive. Public education campaigns are necessary to point out that bicycles, rather than being a nuisance to cars and pedestrians, actually open up parking stalls for drivers, reduce traffic congestion, and improve air quality.[110] [111]

Encouraging More Walking and Cycling

"A bicycle-friendly city has bicycle lanes on all major roads; priority bicycle routes through quiet residential streets; bike racks on all the buses; bicycle-controlled traffic signals; cycling maps; bicycle deliveries; cycling education programs; free electric charging stations for electric bikes; and an active cycling advocacy group. A walkable city puts care into the design of its pedestrian routes, widens the sidewalks, builds sidewalk bulges at intersections, creates open-air pedestrian shopping centers and encourages pedestrian advocacy groups."

– Liz Armstrong, Guy Dauncey, and Anne Wordsworth. 2007. *Cancer: 101 Solutions to a Preventable Epidemic*. New Society Publishers.

MORE INFO
- Car-free — the book: J.H. Crawford. 2000. *Carfree Cities*. International Books.
- Car-free — the website: carfree.com

ZERO-FARE PUBLIC TRANSPORT: THE BELGIAN CITY OF HASSELT

More than 11 years ago, the Belgian city of Hasselt embarked on a bold plan: no fees for local riders.

When Flemish transport minister Eddy Baldewijns created an integrated transport policy framework in 1996, the 70,000-soul city of Hasselt in the Flemish province of Limburg was one of the first to subscribe to the plan. Mayor Steve Stevaert advocated giving priority to public transport in the city's central "Green Boulevard." The Green Boulevard is an inner ring road that keeps the commercial center almost entirely car-free. From 6 am to 7 pm, the Boulevard Shuttle runs at 5-minute intervals, the Central Shuttle runs every 10 minutes, and system-wide wait times are never longer than half an hour until reduced evening services. While bus rides are free for everyone within city limits, the regional bus system is available free of charge only for citizens of Hasselt.

The intent of the program was to make the new bus system the natural option for getting around, and it did. The system saw a 783% increase in ridership on the first day (Figure 5.2).

Two of the four Green Boulevard lanes were closed for cars and made available for bicycles instead.[112, 113, 114]

Costs and Benefits

While buses and trams in the not-too-distant cities of Antwerp and Liège are sitting in traffic jams, almost empty of passengers, the "Hasselt Pilot Model" has become a hallmark of fresh green thinking. Ironically, the project was started because the city was the most bankrupt city in Belgium. Traffic planners advised building a third ring

VOLVO BUS INC.

FIGURE 5.2
Free transit has increased ridership in the City of Hasselt by over 1,100% and contributed to its rating as Belgium's city with the highest standard of living.

road, at a cost of several billion euros. The city currently pays € 1 million per year to the local bus company, or about 1% of the city's annual budget. At the same time, parking rates for the inner city were raised and secured park-and-ride parking spots provided outside the city center free of charge. The province contributes an additional € 5 million a year, a tiny fraction of what it would have to have provided in matching funding for the third ring road.[115, 116]

Hasselt Has Highest Standard of Living

A 2007 study of 20 Belgian cities by the consumer report magazine Testaankoop *awarded Hasselt the status of city with the highest standard of living. The excellent public transit system, bicycle infrastructure, and general contentment of the citizenry were among the top factors cited.*[117]

Ridership in Hasselt went up from 360,000 in 1996 before the introduction of the program to 4,614,844 passengers annually by 2006, an increase of 1,182%.

Free Transit Grows City Economy

A study commissioned by the Belgian Centre for Economic Development credits Hasselt's extensive and free transit system as the primary reason for its meteoric rise to becoming the country's third-most favoured shopping destination.[116]

Since the introduction of the program, Hasselt moved from the tenth-most favored shopping destination to the third-most favored one, increasing inner city employment from 1,000 jobs to 3,000. Rob Beenders, head of Hasselt's transportation department, also attributes the marked increases in tourist visits to the city in part to the free transit system and improved air quality, with hotel space increasing from a single hotel at the start of the program to 1,500 beds currently. Since 90% of Hasselt's citizens are using and benefiting directly from the system, Beenders' city council party has experienced a sharp rise in popularity since the introduction of the new transit structure.[118, 119]

Future Plans

The city is currently planning the addition of a light-rail transit system as well as the introduction of electric buses. Hasselt also plans to purchase only carbon-neutral buses in the future.

MORE INFO
• Wikipedia: en.wikipedia.org/wiki/Public_transport_in_Hasselt
  QuickLink: CarbonCharter.org/18

PLUG-IN HYBRID VEHICLES

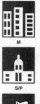

Plug-in hybrid electric vehicles (PHEVs) are cars and trucks that are enabled to operate in all-electric mode for up to 90 to 100% of daily driving, including commuting to work, shopping, and picking up kids.

Advantages of plug-in hybrids include greatly reduced driving costs, with the equivalent of less than 62¢/gallon (16¢ /liter) for some PHEVs, and vastly reduced carbon emissions. Even electricity from carbon-intensive coal-fired power plants results in gas-powered cars having 34% lower CO_2 emissions, due to the high efficiency of electric motors. Furthermore, plug-in hybrids can be recharged from renewable electric sources such as wind or photovoltaics, for potentially 100% carbon-reduced rides.[120]

PHEVs from retrofits, or those shortly coming onto the market, have ranges from 35 to 180 miles (about 55 to 290 km).

Interestingly, 80% of US drivers travel less than 40 miles (60 km) per day: all of this driving could be powered by electricity alone, while the internal combustion engine (ICE) could still be used for longer trips when desired.[121]

The embodied energy of the extra battery packs is expected to add about 2% to the lifecycle energy costs of PHEVs compared to hybrids and about 4% compared to regular cars while reducing lifecycle carbon emissions between 40 and 90% during operation. The incremental cost of hybrid technology is about US$2,500 per car, and an additional estimated US$3,000 for PHEV technology in mass production.

Some cities are planning to introduce public recharge stations for PHEVs. Another long-term benefit of PHEVs is their potential ability to even out utility company peak demands through a concept called "Vehicle-to-Grid" (V2G), under which PHEV owners could sell excess battery capacity back to the utility during times of peak demand (e.g., summer air conditioning at noon) and benefit from the higher electricity spot price during high demand for electricity. Car owners may move from owning a car that costs them $2,000 in gas per year to one that earns them $3,000 from electricity trading, even if the car is parked in the garage. Utility companies, on the other hand, would benefit from a large reservoir of extra capacity during peak hours.[122] [123]

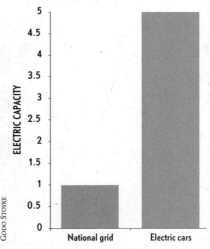

FIGURE 5.3
A conversion of 2 million Danish cars to electric mode would provide reserve capacity exceeding the Danish national electrical grid requirements by a factor of five.

Denmark recently signed up for an electric car infrastructure to be built in conjunction with Californian company Better Place betterplace.com. With 20%, Denmark

INCREMENTAL			YEAR 1	YEAR 2	YEAR 3	YEAR 4	YEAR 5
	Car 1	embodied	12.0				
		operation	8.0	8.0	8.0	8.0	8.0
			20.0	28.0	36.0	44.0	5.2
	PHEV	embodied	16.0				
		operation	0	0	0	0	0
			16.0	16.0	16.0	16.0	16.0
	Prius	embodied	14.0				
		operation	5.2	5.2	5.2	5.2	5.2
			19.2	24.4	29.6	34.8	40.0
energy payback	Prius		0.96				
energy payback	PHEV		0.8				

FIGURE 5.4
Reduction in operational carbon emissions of Toyota Prius with Hymotion PHEV retrofit while in full-electric mode.[102, 125]

has the highest percentage of renewably supplied electricity, most of it coming from wind turbines. It has been estimated that two million electric cars in Denmark could supply five times as much electricity as the whole national grid under a V2G scenario (Figure 5.3). Other jurisdictions that have signed up for Better Place's infrastructure include Israel, Australia, Hawaii, and the Californian municipalities of San Francisco, San Jose, and Oakland.[124] According to a study by the Electric Power Research Institute (EPRI) and the Natural Resources Defense Council (NRDC), widespread adoption of PHEVs in the US alone would reduce carbon emissions equivalent to taking 82.5 million cars off the road (Figure 5.4).[126]

Former CIA director R. James Woolsey is a supporter of PHEVs for reasons of national security since they would largely end the dependence on imported oil, and

FIGURE 5.5
The Chevy Volt is the first plug-in hybrid announced by one of the three large American automakers.

© GM CORP.

GODO STOYKE

oil, period.[127] A US Department of Energy study found that up to 80% of all cars could be powered by the electrical grid without adding production capacity if the current fleet were converted to PHEVs.

Both GM with its Chevy Volt and Toyota with its revamped Prius vehicle have announced plans to introduce mass-produced PHEVs in the near future (Figure 5.5).

MORE INFO

- Book: Sherry Boschert. 2006. *Plug-in Hybrids: The Cars That Will Recharge America.* New Society Publishers.
- Mailing list of Calcars, a non-profit promoter of PHEVs: calcars-newsowner@yahoo groups. com; website: calcars.org
- After-market conversion of Toyota Prius to PHEV status (fleet and individual conversions available since 2008): a123systems. com/hymotion
- North America's first serially produced PHEVs (2009 for electric, early 2010 for PHEV version): aptera.com
- Chevrolet Volt PHEV expected in 2010: chevrolet.com/ electriccar/
- Toyota Prius PHEV expected in 2011: blog.toyota.com/ 2008/01/what-are-all-th.html
- The world's first commercially available PHEV, the F3DM, was released on December 15, 2008, by Chinese firm BYD: byd.com. It costs over 40% less than the Toyota Prius in China.

Examples and Case Studies: Plug-in Austin

Under the direction of Austin City Council, the City of Austin and Austin Energy are leading members of "Plug-in Partners," a US national campaign to convince car manufacturers that there is a sufficient market for PHEVs to make them economically worthwhile (Figure 5.6).

In March of 2005, Roger Duncan, Deputy General Manager, Distributed Energy Services, and Michael J. Osborne, Austin Energy, submitted a report on "transportation convergence" in response to City of Austin Council Resolution 040729-78 calling for a report on the convergence of the electricity and transportation sectors and its potential impact on Austin Energy.

The report proposed a utility rebate program for PHEVs and a move by municipal and other local government agencies to indicate a willingness to purchase PHEVs in the future.

In response to the report, 600 national partners signed on, including the 50 largest cities, to convince car manufacturers that there is a PHEV market. Partly as a result of this initiative, all major car manufacturers now have PHEV programs and there are federal tax credits for PHEV purchase and tax incentives for battery manufacturers.[128, 129, 130]

MORE INFO

- Report on Transportation Convergence prepared for the City of Austin: pluginpartners.org/includes/pdfs/gasOptionalvehicles.pdf
- Austin Energy website on PHEVs: austinenergy.com/About %20Us/Environmental%20Initiatives/Plug-in%20Hybrid%20 Vehicles/index.htm
  QuickLink: CarbonCharter.org/19

FIGURE 5.6
The City of Austin and Austin Energy have become leading members in the US national "Plug-in Partners" campaign.

CONGESTION AND CO₂ CHARGES

Congestion Charge

A levy raised for entering high density areas of a city by car.

Purpose and Benefits

The aims of congestion charges are to reduce car traffic in congested city cores, to raise money for transportation infrastructure costs, to encourage the use of public transit, and to reduce carbon emissions.

Examples and Case Studies: London Congestion Charge

One of the most widely copied congestion charges came into effect in Central London on February 17, 2003, promoted by then-mayor of London, Ken Livingstone. Cars entering the highly congested Central London area are now charged £8 (about US$ 16) per day. The fee was introduced with the addition of 300 new buses to expand public transit access. Handicapped drivers are exempt (Figure 5.7).

FIGURE 5.7
A congestion charge was introduced for downtown London in 2003.

CO₂ Charge

Beginning in October 2008, the Central London congestion charge was going to be based on CO₂ emissions of cars, with higher fees of £25 for vehicles emitting more than 225g CO_2/km traveled (approximately equivalent to using more than 9 l/100 km or getting less than 24 miles per gallon) and a 100% discount for cars with emissions equivalent to getting more than 50 miles per gallon (5 l/100 km or less). (The new mayor of London has put the implementation of the CO_2 charge on hold.)

Results

The results of the initiative were as follows:

The average number of cars and delivery vehicles entering the central zone was 60,000 fewer than in the previous year. Around 50 to 60% of this reduction was attributed to transfers to public transport, 20 to 30% to journeys avoiding the zone, 15 to 25% to switching to car share, and the remainder to a reduction in the number of journeys taken, to more traveling outside the hours of operation, and to an increased use of motorbikes and bicycles. Journey times were found to have been reduced by 14%.[131, 132]

Other Jurisdictions

Other jurisdictions that have adopted a congestion charge include Singapore (1975), Rome (1998), Stockholm (2006; Figure 5.8), and Valletta (2007).[131, 133, 134, 135]

KINGDOM OF SWEDEN

FIGURE 5.8
Swedish congestion charge road sign.

MORE INFO

• City of London, CO_2 charge: tfl.gov.uk/roadusers/congestioncharging/7394.aspx
 QuickLink: CarbonCharter.org/20

RENEWABLE ENERGY

FEED-IN TARIFFS

Feed-in Tariffs

Financial incentives offered to providers of renewable electrici-
ty fed into the public utility grid. Also called FiT, FiL, Feed-in
Law, solar premium, renewable tariff.

Purpose and Benefits

THE AIMS OF FEED-IN TARIFFS ARE TO ENCOURAGE THE INSTALLATION
of added renewable electrical capacity, usually including solar electricity (photovoltaics), wind power, biomass, and geothermal power, by
mandating a government-proscribed premium to energy providers,
which has to be borne by the customers of the utility company.

Examples and Case Studies: Germany's Renewable Energy Act (EEG)

The Renewable Energy Act (Erneuerbare-Energien-Gesetz or EEG)
is widely considered one of the earliest and most successful feed-in

79

tariff laws and has been adopted in some form by 47 countries.[136]

The EEG had its origins in a 1989 market stimulation program that guaranteed a fixed payment per kWh of electricity produced, and also provided incentives for private operators such as farmers. This program was in effect until 1995. In 1991, an additional program was introduced: the Electricity Feed-in Act. It mandated that grid operators pay 80% of average retail prices to producers of renewable energy as an incentive. These two programs led to the first boom in renewable energy production in Germany, particularly for wind energy, which tended to provide the most cost-effective source of renewable energy. This is why the early programs came to be known as the *Windpfennig* (extra penny for wind).

The program coincided with electricity deregulation, so that the feed-in was later capped at 5% of grid consumption to prevent great disparity in grid operator pricing. However, due to feed-in prices being tied to variable electrical retail rates, economic remuneration for wind turbine operators was uncertain and increased economic risks.

In 2000, the Renewable Energy Act replaced the Electricity Feed-in Act. Now, feed-in prices were no longer linked to retail prices but fixed for 20 years, guaranteeing investors a predictable and safe return. Also, the costs of renewables were now spread across the country-wide grid.[137]

Starting in 2002, tariffs also included a "degression," a predetermined decrease in guaranteed feed-in tariffs over time for new installations, to encourage reductions in system installation costs. The expiration date for the feed-in tariffs for each installation was set at 20 years.

The tariffs were also stepped, so that, for example, feed-in tariffs at high-quality wind sites that exceeded reference levels had a more substantial degression after five years than those at below-par sites since paybacks at these sites could be reached more quickly even without incentives.

The goal of the EEG of 2000 was to double the production of renewable electricity by 2010.

Amendments in 2004 adjusted feed-in tariff rates for different renewable technologies, installation sizes, and locations. For example, higher tariffs were provided for geothermal and solar electricity as well as for certain forms of energy production from biomass. Smaller biomass plants as well as smaller biogas plants from landfills received relatively higher tariffs. The same was done for offshore wind, the goal being to accelerate development of this relatively newer renewable energy source.[136] [137] [138]

FIGURE 6.1
The component of green energy in Germany's electrical mix has risen from 3% to 14% since the introduction of feed-in tariffs in 1989.

In addition to the German Federal Environment Ministry (BMU), which administers most of the program, other departments have also provided incentives. For example, the Ministry of Agriculture plays a special role in biomass development, and the Bank for Reconstruction and Development provides loans at reduced rates for renewables and energy efficiency.

Costs and Benefits of the EEG

In 1990, renewables generated 3% of Germany's electrical production. By 2007, the EEG and its predecessors had increased the renewable component to 14.2%, far ahead of the rate targeted at the introduction of the EEG (12.5% by 2010; Figure 6.1).[138, 139]

It is believed that the EEG was the principal creator of about 250,000 renewable energy jobs in Germany in 2007 and that these will grow to at least 500,000 by 2020, and possibly 800,000 by 2030.

More than 80% of German wind turbine production is exported, though photovoltaic installation still exceeds national production.[138]

Windpfennig

"As a result of Germany's Renewable Energy Act of 1999, which includes a feed-in policy, renewable energy jobs are up to 200,000, renewable energy is at 12% of total energy production, and annual installation of solar PV systems exceeds those in all other countries combined."

~ Sarah van Gelder, "13 Best Energy Ideas"[141]

Other Jurisdictions

For a summary of current feed-in tariffs from a variety of jurisdictions from around the world, see Figure 6.2.

MORE INFO

• Summary of the Renewable Energy Act (EEG): bmu.de/english/renewable_energy/doc/6465.php

First Year Renewable Tariffs in US$/kWh Exchange rates are for July 12, 2008

			$US/KWH		
	WIND	PV	HYDRO	BIOGAS	OFFSHORE WIND
Austria	0.012	0.724		0.267	
Brazil	0.087		0.061	0.077	
California		0.500			
Czech Republic	0.136	0.729			
France	0.132	0.877	0.086	0.142	0.047-0.204
Germany 2008	0.126	0.736	0.116	0.170	0.055-0.22
Italy		0.866			
Minnesota C-BED	0.048				
Ontario	0.108	0.413	0.108	0.108	
Portugal	0.124		0.129		
South Korea		0.891			
Spain (2007 RD)	0.119	0.716		0.213	0.137
Turkey	0.079				
Washington State		0.540			

FIGURE 6.2
First-year renewable feed-in tariffs from around the world. Adapted from Paul Gipe's website wind-works.org.

- Complete text of the Renewable Energy Act (EEG): bmu.de/files/pdfs/allgemein/application/pdf/eeg_en.pdf
- The GRU in Gainesville, Florida was the first US municipal owned utility introducing a German-style solar power feed-in tariff in 2009: gru.com/OurEnvironment/GreenEnergy/solar.jsp treehugger.com/files/2009/02/solar-power-feed-in-tariff-approved-gainesville-florida.php

RESOURCES

- Paul Gipe, one of the leading writers on all aspects of wind turbines, provides detailed information on feed-in tariffs from around the world on his website at wind-works.org/articles/feed _laws. html#What%20are%20ARTs?.
  QuickLink: CarbonCharter.org/21

What is the Role of Nuclear Energy in Abating Climate Change?

The Environment Ministry of the German government provides the following reasons for Germany's decision for a scheduled shutdown of its nuclear power plants:

Will nuclear power ensure climate protection?

Even though nuclear power emits no greenhouse gases at the station, the mining and refining of the uranium fuel results in the release of 31 to 61 grams (1 to 2 ounces) of CO_2e per kilowatt-hour (kWh). This is less than emissions from fossil fuels, but more than emissions from renewables, e.g., wind power at 23 grams (2/3 of an ounce) released during turbine manufacture.

A sustainable energy source?

Nuclear power results in highly radioactive nuclear waste that is a danger for millenia. There is not a single approved long-term storage site anywhere in the world. Supposedly safe storage in salt mines, for example at Asse, Germany, has been found to be compromised by infiltration of water, which destabilizes the storage site. A tenet of "sustainability" is that our actions must not negatively affect the quality of life of future generations. Economically accessible uranium fuel is expected to last 65 years at current consumption (much less if nuclear programs were expanded significantly), yet guarding radioactive waste will be a concern for hundreds of future generations. Extending the useful life of fuel through "fast breeders" would result in highly toxic plutonium and create weapons-grade material.

Is nuclear energy cost-effective?

Nuclear electricity is at least twice as costly as electricity derived from fossil sources.

After a slight increase in the number of operating nuclear reactors from 423 to 444 between 1989 and 2002, the number has since dropped to 439. Not a single reactor can be built without vast government subsidies.

The supposed nuclear renaissance is the attempt by a few companies to extract the maximum amount of public subsidies for an aging and unsustainable technology.[140]

[Nuclear energy is also significantly more expensive than wind power. Solar electricity (photovoltaics or PV) is still significantly more expensive than nuclear power; however, unlike nuclear plants which will be competing for increasingly costly uranium, photovoltaic installations have been steadily getting less expensive, even without the massive research subsidies that have been granted to nuclear electricity generation in the past. The Deutsche Bank estimates that PV without subsidies will reach cost-parity with fossil sources in much of the US by 2011 to 2015.[142]]

RENEWABLE INCENTIVE PROGRAMS

Berkeley FIRST

Purpose and Benefits

Berkeley FIRST (Financing Initiative for Renewable and Solar Technology) is a program being developed by the City of Berkeley

CITY OF BERKELEY

FIGURE 6.3
In 2008, the Californian City of Berkeley piloted the "BerkeleyFIRST" program, which allows homeowners to obtain solar collectors and panels, as well as efficiency retrofits, at no up-front costs. These are paid for through increased tax bills over 20 years (image shows Mayor Tom Bates presenting the proposal in November of 2007).

that provides residential and commercial property owners access to funding for solar electric and thermal systems as well as for efficiency improvements.

The program was invented by the city's former chief of staff, Cisco DeVries, in early 2007, proposed by the Mayor in October, and approved unanimously by council in November of the same year (Figure 6.3).

The cost for the installation program, including interest, is paid through an annual special tax on the owner's property tax bill over 20 years.[143, 144, 145, 146]

The US Environmental Protection Agency contributed US$160,000 to the city to offset the legal and administrative fees for the initial setup.

The advantage of the system is that property owners incur no up-front cost for reducing the energy costs and environmental impact of their buildings and do not have to continue to pay for the cost if they sell their property; nor does it affect the owner's credit rating. Additionally, the city can typically get lower interest rates on the initial loan than individual property owners.

Property owners are expected to save as much in energy costs as they would be paying in taxes.[144]

Details of the Program

The Berkeley FIRST program was piloted in 2008 and is intended to be made available to all residents once a successful pilot has been completed.

Currently, a California city has to be a "charter city" to implement a program of this kind. In California, 108 out of 478 cities are charter cities. Legislation has been introduced to amend state law to allow all cities in California to set up this program.

In 2008, Berkeley city council approved an amendment to the Berkeley Municipal Code (BMC) to create the Special Tax Financing Law that incorporates by reference the provisions of the state's Mello-Roos Act. The Special Tax Financing Law is the implementing legislation that allows the creation of a Sustainable Energy Financing District.

The initiative is a contribution to the city's 2006 Measure G mandate, which was overwhelmingly endorsed by Berkeley voters via ballot and would see the city reduce its greenhouse gas emissions by 80% by 2050.

Berkeley has committed to create a replication guide for other cities after their pilot phase is completed.[143] [145]

It is interesting to note that Berkeley has a long history of passing prescient and innovative sustainability bylaws and resolutions, including the following:

Procurement Policies:

1983: Local Business Preference[147]

1990: Preference for Recycled Paper[148]

2003: Adoption of the "Precautionary Principle"[149]

2004: Environmental Preferable Purchasing (10% price preference)[150]

2006: Extension of the "Precautionary Principle"[151]

Other Sustainable Ordinances:

2003: LEED® Silver for municipal buildings[152]

2005: Support for Kyoto Protocol[153]

2005: Zero Waste Goal[154]

2007: Renewable Energy Purchase Program for building owners paid out of property taxes (Berkeley FIRST)

All ordinances are available at cityofberkeley.info/Content Display.aspx?id=15538.

For general sustainability initiatives of the City of Berkeley, please visit cityofberkeley.info/sustainable.

MORE INFO
• To subscribe to Berkeley FIRST updates, enter your email address at service.govdelivery.com/service/action/subscribe? code= CABERKE_9.

RESOURCES
• An FAQ on the program is available at ci.berkeley.ca.us/mayor//GHG/SEFD-FAQ.htm.
  QuickLink: CarbonCharter.org/22

RENEWABLE HEATING

Purpose and Benefits

The use of renewable heating reduces greenhouse gas emissions and ensures a sustainable and secure energy supply.

Examples and Case Studies: Germany's Renewable Energies Heat Act (EEWärmeG)

Highlights of the Act

The Renewable Energies Heat Act came into effect on January 1, 2009, and regulates the use of renewable energy for heating and cooling in all new building construction. The Act has three components:

1. The mandatory use of renewables for the heating and cooling of all new buildings. Renewables, for the purpose of the Act, include ground-source heat pumps ("geothermal"), air-source heat pumps, thermal solar collection, biomass (solid, liquid, or gas, including methane from sanitary landfills and sewage), and plant oil methyl esters ("biodiesel"). Waste heat from exhaust air and sewage as well as cogeneration (also known as combined-heat-and-power, or CHP) and district heating systems can be used as a

FIGURE 6.4
Solar heating is one of the options to meet the requirements for new buildings under the German Renewable Energies Heat Act that became law in January of 2009.

"substitute" measure under the act. In total, the renewable and substitute measures must provide 100% of the building's space heating and cooling and domestic hot water needs (Figure 6.4).

2. The federal government provides financial incentives for the use of renewables in new building construction from 2009 to 2012 of up to € 500 million (about US$750 million) annually (only solar, biomass, and heat pumps are eligible for the incentives). Measures are eligible if they exceed the percentages described in "Details of the EEWärmeG" (below) or increase the energy efficiency of the building.

3. The Act allows local authorities to mandate the hookup of local buildings to a district heating system to guarantee economy of scale.

Details of the EEWärmeG

Here is a run-down of the highlights of the EEWärmeG that came into force in January of 2009:

To meet the requirements of the Act, the renewables must meet a minimum of the space heating and domestic hot water needs of any new building as follows:

- solar heating must meet a minimum of 15% of the building's heating needs
- gaseous biomass a minimum of 30%
- liquid and solid biomass a minimum of 50%
- heat pumps (air or ground-source) a minimum of 50%
- Cogeneration and district heating systems must meet a minimum of 50%.

Exceptions are made for cases where the use of renewables is not possible and for building types that are not considered suitable for renewables, e.g., tents, greenhouses, homes smaller than 50 m^2 (550 sq. ft.), subterranean buildings, large churches, and certain industrial facilities, or where the Act would place an extraordinary economic burden on the owner.

For solar collectors, the minimum requirements are considered to be met if there are at least

- 0.04 m² (0.32 sq. ft.) of collector surface per m² (10.7 sq. ft.) of living space in a building containing no more than two dwellings, or

- 0.03 m² (0.43 sq. ft.) of collector surface per m² (10.7 sq. ft.) of living space in a building containing more than two dwellings.

Building owners must keep records of gaseous and liquid biomass fuel delivery for 5 years, and of solid biomass fuels for 15 years after use for inspection (similar to an IRS tax audit). Local authorities are required to confirm compliance with the Act, at least through auditing of a sufficient sample size of approved buildings. They are authorized to enter occupied buildings for this purpose, if required.

Non-compliance with the Act by building owners can result in a fine of up to € 50,000 (approx. US$75,000).

The federal government is required to present parliament with a progress report on the Act every four years. This report must review the technical and economic development of renewable technologies, the achieved savings in heating oil and natural gas (the standard heating fuels in Germany), the resulting reductions in greenhouse gas emissions, and the implementation of the Act, and also suggest improvements for the Act.[155]

MORE INFO
- Summary of Germany's Renewable Energies Heat Act (in English): bmu.de/files/pdfs/allgemein/application/pdf/ee_waer megesetz_fragen_en.pdf
- Complete text of the Act (in German): bgblportal.de/BGBL/ bgbl1f/bgbl108s1658.pdf
- More detailed information (in German): erneuerbare-energien.de/inhalt/41719/
  QuickLink: CarbonCharter.org/23

BIODIVERSITY

NEXT TO CLIMATE CHANGE, THE RAPID GLOBAL LOSS OF BIODIVER-sity is probably the second biggest global environmental issue of the century.

Speaking in the Indonesian capital of Jakarta, the UK's Prince Charles recently called for "rainforest bills," referring to rainforests as the "world's greatest public utility" since they act as an air conditioner, store fresh water, and provide work: "Indonesia and the other rainforest nations are stewards of the world's greatest public utility. The rest of us have to start paying for it, just as we pay for our water, gas, and electricity. In return, the rainforest nations would provide eco-services such as carbon storage, fresh water and the protection of biodiversity." According to Prince Charles, the forests used to provide a livelihood for more than a billion people, and since the developed nations through their demand for products like beef, palm oil, soy, and logs were the driving force behind their destruction, they should be billed for their protection (Figure 7.1).[156]

SIMON GURNEY – STOCKEXPERT

FIGURE 7.1
Rainforests have been referred to as the "world's greatest public utility" by the UK's Prince Charles, since they act as air conditioners, store fresh water, and provide sustainable food sources.

THE GLOBAL BIO-BOUNTY AND BIO-FEEBATE

Another option for monetizing biodiversity through market systems is the use of a "bio-bounty" or "bio-feebate." A bio-bounty represents a reward for maintaining the native plant biodiversity of private property, offering reductions in property taxes based on vegetation levels. A bio-feebate combines the carrot with the stick, offering incentives for keeping land highly biodiversified, and increasing tax rates for lands devoid of native plant cover, resulting in a revenue-neutral but effective system for safeguarding biodiversity. (The "feebate" concept was developed in the 1990s by the Rocky Mountain Institute [rmi.org], a resource efficiency think-tank.[157]

How Would This Work?

Here is an example of how the bio-feebate approach could work:

All properties on which more than 25% of the land area has

been converted to land use that does not reflect native vegetation (native vegetation being defined as vegetation for the area believed to have been in existence at the site in the year 1800, or expected to have been in existence at the site in the year 1800 in the absence of human intervention) are subject to bio-feebate taxation, with a limited bonus for instances of carbon storage and green roofs using non-native vegetation. Properties that contain more than 25% of native vegetation are eligible to receive a bio-bounty (biodiversity bounty). Bio-levies for land with less than 25% of native vegetation shall represent 5% of property values in 2010, 10% of property values in 2015, and 20% of property values in 2020. Provisions are made to permit the continued use of agriculture, i.e., rates for historic agricultural areas are reduced. Bio-bounties and bio-taxes shall be levied as property taxes.

Bio-bounties and bio-taxes on government lands shall be levied as internationally tradeable bio-credits. Bio-levies (bounties and taxes) shall be approximately revenue-neutral in sum in the first year of operation. Standards for levies shall be increased in severity

JOSEPH LUOMAN – ISTOCKPHOTO

FIGURE 7.2
Under a bio-feebate system, areas denuded of native vegetation incur higher property taxes.

every five years to move towards increased sustainability and bio-diversity (Figure 7.2).

Food Production in Cities

Food production in cities can remove the pressure from the surrounding countryside and provide fresher food for city dwellers while reducing transport costs.

Ways to increase food production in cities include

- *community gardens,*
- *roof-top gardens, and*
- *permaculture (edible landscaping) in public spaces.*

QuickLink: CarbonCharter.org/24

INTEGRATED
MUNICIPAL DESIGN

DISTRICT HEATING AND COOLING
DESIGN: HAMMARBY SJÖSTAD

HAMMARBY SJÖSTAD IS A NEW DISTRICT IN THE MUNICIPALITY OF
Stockholm, Sweden, at 59° latitude north, where the city has
imposed advanced requirements on buildings, installations, and traffic systems from day one. Planning for the district began in 1990,
and it is expected to house over 25,000 people upon completion in
2015. The goal of Hammarby Sjöstad's environmental program is to
halve the total environmental impact compared to that of a regular
district built in the early '90s.[158] This is Stockholm's biggest development project in recent years. It is located in a former industrial and
port area (brownfield development; Figures 8.1, 8.2).

District heating is the main source of heating in Hammarby
Sjöstad, and since 2002, nearly 100% of it has been supplied from
renewable sources, including 34% of the heat extracted from treated wastewater, 47% from combustible household waste, and 16%
from biofuel. The same district heating system also provides district cooling (Figure 8.3).[159, 160]

FIGURE 8.1
Walkways connect Hammarby Sjöstad neighborhoods.

Some of the other interesting environmental features of the development include the following:

Nature Conservation

• Existing vegetation has been protected where possible during construction, some areas were revegetated, and some dead trees (snags) were left behind on purpose to provide habitat for specific bird and insect species.

• Ecoducts (planted viaducts over the highway) connect the nearby Nacka nature reserve with the town, and

FIGURE 8.2
The word "Sjöstad" in the second half of the district's name means "lake city."

FIGURE 8.3
District-wide energy systems can provide both heating and cooling for urban buildings.

provide pleasant footpaths for pedestrians as well as dispersal corridors for animal and plant species (Figure 8.4).

Open Space Standards and Access to Sunlight

- There shall be at least 15 m²/165 sq. ft. of courtyard space and a total of 25 to 30 m²/275 to 330 sq. ft. of courtyard space and park area within 300 m/1,000 feet of every apartment, or the equivalent of 100 m²/11,000 sq. ft. of living space.[160]
- At least 5 % of the courtyard space shall be sunlit for at least 4 to 5 hours at the spring and autumn equinoxes.[160]

Water Policies

- To prevent contamination of rainwater, all facades, roofing materials, and footpaths must be free of heavy metals and other toxic substances. An environmentally friendly oil was used on the footpaths along Sickla Canal, and stainless steel for the cycle bridge.

MJPO.NL/FAUNAPASSAGES/ECODUCTEN

FIGURE 8.4
Planted viaducts over highways, or "ecoducts," provide pleasant pedestrian footpaths as well as dispersal corridors for native plant and animal species.

- To save water, high-efficiency (European class A) washing machines and dishwashers have been installed as well as low-flush toilets and air mixer taps, dropping consumption from the average 200 l/53 gallons per person per day in Stockholm to 150 l/40 gallons in Hammarby Sjöstad. The long-term goal is to drop the consumption by an additional 50 l/13 gallons per person per day. (For comparison, US consumption is 638 l/169 gallons per person per day.)
- 95% of phosphorous in wastewater is being reused in agriculture.
- Wastewater targets are 23 mg/gallon (6 mg/l) for nitrogen and 0.57 mg/gallon (0.15 mg/l) for phosphorous.

Materials Policy
- Pressure-treated lumber is not permitted.
- Exterior galvanized materials must be surface-treated.
- Recycled construction materials are preferred.

Waste Reduction

- All construction waste must be sorted on-site.
- Recyclable materials are presorted in households, including solid waste suitable as a feedstock for the cogeneration plant and organic waste used for biofuel (Figure 8.5).

Energy

- In addition to the biofuel generation from organic waste and sewage, cogeneration and district heating, heat extraction from treated sewage, and use of solid waste for cogeneration (see above and below), some solar (photovoltaic) cells are used for electricity production, and 390 m^2/4,300 sq. ft. of solar hot water collectors have been installed.
- Upon completion, residents will produce half of all the energy they need. Renewable sources will provide 100% of the heating energy and 100% of the electricity.
- Stockholm's district heating system is now the largest in the world.

Planning, Integrated Design, and Eco-industrial Design

- Hammarby Sjöstad represents a unique partnership between the city administration, architects, developers, and local utility companies right from the start of the project.
- The integrated design (called "eco-cycle" at Hammarby Sjöstad) displays many characteristics of an eco-industrial park, where the waste product from one

HEMERA TECHNOLOGIES INC.

FIGURE 8.5
Recycling is only the first step in a closed-system product loop. The next step is incorporating recycled materials into new products.

process serves as a feedstock for another (Figure 8.6). For example, combustible waste and biofuels power the Högdalen cogeneration (or combined heat and power [CHP]) plant. The

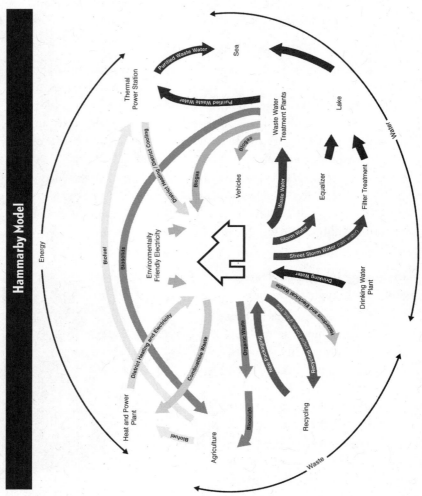

FIGURE 8.6
Eco-cycle (eco-industrial cycle) of Hammarby's energy, water, and waste. Many waste products of one process become the resource- and energy-efficient feedstock of the next process.

cogeneration plant creates renewable electricity, and the waste heat in turn is supplied as heating energy to homes. Sewage is used to create biofuel, and heat is also extracted by the Hammarby plant from the treated wastewater coming from the Henriksdal wastewater treatment plant to supply heating energy to the buildings. The cooled-down wastewater is used via heat pumps to feed into the district cooling network. A full 95% of phosphorous in wastewater is recaptured for agricultural use (Figure 8.7). Lifecycle analysis is being carried out to determine the sustainability of recapturing nitrogen chemical energy from wastewater for agricultural use.

DAN SHIRLEY – STOCKXCHNG IMAGE

FIGURE 8.7
In Hammarby Sjöstad, nutrients are extracted from household sewage to supply agricultural processes.

- Hammarby Sjöstad receives visits from over 10,000 city councillors and specialists from around the world each year.

- GlashusEtt is a local environmental information center for national and international visitors. It also serves as a venue for workshops and exhibits and passes on the information gained at Hammarby Sjöstad to other municipalities. GlashusEtt is funded by the Stockholm Water Company, Fortum, the Stockholm district energy company, and the Stockholm Development Office.[160]

Waste

Waste in Hammarby Sjöstad is no longer treated as pollution but as a resource. The district has a three-level waste management system: building-based, block-based, and area-based. The building-based system separates waste at the source and allows for collection of the heaviest and bulkiest waste: combustible waste and food waste can be deposited in different chutes near the apartment buildings. The block-based recycling rooms deal with paper, metal, glass, and plastic packaging. The area-based recycling center collects hazardous waste, including solvents and electronics.

Future Goals

By 2010, Hammarby Sjöstad expects to extract energy from 99% by weight of all domestic waste that has an extractable energy content. [161] Extensive investments are being made in developing a green transportation infrastructure, and by 2010 the district expects 80% of local and commuter trips to be made by public transport, on foot, or by bicycle. Hammarby Sjöstad has a light rail link from Alvik, bus routes to Stockholm city, a year-round ferry system, and a car-sharing program open to any resident or local employee, currently with 350 members and 35 cars. So far, 75 % of the car-sharing vehicles run on biofuel, and the target is for 15% of the households to join the program by 2010. [158, 160]

MORE INFO
- Municipal website of Hammarby Sjöstad: hammarbysjostad.se
- Address of the environmental information center GlashusEtt: GlashusEtt, Lugnets allé 39, SE-120 66 Stockholm, Sweden hammarbysjostad.se/frameset.asp?target=inenglish/inenglish _glashusett.asp
QuickLink: CarbonCharter.org/25

SYMBIOCITY: THE SHORT TERM IS OBSOLETE

Examples of integrated and sustainable municipal design are so rife in Sweden that the country has launched a website specifically dedicated to showcasing examples of Swedish municipal sustainable design and technologies. The symbiocity.org site was unveiled by Maud Olofsson, Sweden's Deputy Prime Minister, at the Washington Convention Center on March 4, 2008.

Although the SymbioCity concept is Swedish in origin, its components have already been applied throughout the world, in countries ranging from Canada, Ireland, the UK, France, and Russia to India, South Africa, and China.

The section "District Heating and Cooling Design: Hammarby Sjöstad" (above) describes one version of the SymbioCity approach. Other aspects of this approach include the integration of the following measures during planning and construction: rainwater collection, access to public transit, the siting of industrial zones, the fermentation of biodegradable waste, the production of biogas from biomass, and the attenuation of stormwater through attractive open ponds with varying water levels. Yet another feature of the SymbioCity concept involves the education of school children through the use of green spaces.

The SymbioCity website is designed to facilitate the exchange of over 700 Swedish sustainability consultants, contractors, and suppliers with countries around the world. The site provides Swedish cleantech contacts for projects ranging from bioenergy to sustainable buildings.

MORE INFO
- The Symbiocity website is at symbiocity.org.
- The SymbioCity brochure is available at symbiocity.org/download/SymbioCity_24p_brochure_V1.pdf.
- Specific cleantech company contacts can be found at symbio city.org/default.aspx?pageId=6.
- Swedish Trade Council:
  Swedish Trade Council — SymbioCity
  Telephone: +46 8 588 660 00
  E-mail: symbiocity@swedishtrade.se
  QuickLink: CarbonCharter.org/26

WASTE

Waste Reduction for Homes in Stockholm in 2008

"Less than 20% of household waste in Sweden today is deposited as landfill. —— In Stockholm, 75% of all waste is collected for recycling or use as fuel. For household waste, this figure is 95%!"

~ Swedish Trade Council [162]

SWEDISH CITIES ARE TAKING THE OLD CONCEPT OF WASTE AND turning it into a feedstock for energy and biofuel in an eco-industrial loop (see pp. 95-102). A number of American cities have adopted "zero-waste" targets for solid waste.

Zero-Waste Planning

"Twenty-five years ago, many solid waste planners thought no more than 15% to 20% of the municipal waste stream could be recycled. Today numerous communities have surpassed 50% recycling, and many individual establishments — public and private sector — such as office buildings, schools, hospitals, restaurants, and supermarkets have approached 90% and higher levels."

~ Institute for Local Self-Reliance [163]

Municipal examples from around the world include:

- Canberra, Australia, was the first large city to adopt a zero-waste plan, aiming to eliminate the city's two landfills by 2010 and replacing them with "recycling estates."
- San Francisco passed a Zero Waste Resolution that was adopted by the San Francisco Commission on the Environment on April 16, 2002.
- In 1998, the City of Seattle adopted a new plan to recycle 60% of all the waste generated in Seattle by 2008.
- Berkeley adopted a Zero Waste Goal in 2005.[154]

See "Integrated Municipal Design" (p. 95) for further examples of waste reduction.

MORE INFO
- San Francisco Zero Waste: sfenvironment.org/our_programs/overview.html?ssi=3
- Seattle Solid Waste Plan: ci.seattle.wa.us/, search "solid waste plan"
- Institute for Local Self-Reliance: ilsr.org/recycling/zerowaste/index.html
QuickLink: CarbonCharter.org/27

A CARBON-FREE SOCIETY

THE STORY SO FAR

THE EXAMPLES IN THIS BOOK HAVE SHOWN THAT WE ALREADY possess the pieces of the puzzle to move to a carbon-free society if implemented consistently. Växjö (p. 32) .increased its renewable heating supply from 39% to 77% in ten years (Figure 10.1), Berkeley's BerkeleyFIRST program (p. 84) shows how we can rapidly increase our energy efficiency and our utilization of solar energy and energy efficiency, and Austin's plug-in hybrid proposal (p. 74) addresses the issue of our transportation emissions. Remarkably, once institutional inertia is overcome and an economy of scale is reached, most of the sustainability solutions are cheaper than their unsustainable alternatives, even before the large costs of climate change are calculated into cost-benefit analyses. China's introduction of the US$22,000 BYD F3DM plug-in hybrid (PHEV, p. 71) shows that in the future car manufacturers will have to compete on price as well as technology in the sustainability field, moving hybrid and plug-in hybrid availability from the eco-elite to the masses. PHEVs and electric cars are the only technologies required

Energy Supply for Heating 1993 and 2003
(electric heating is not included)

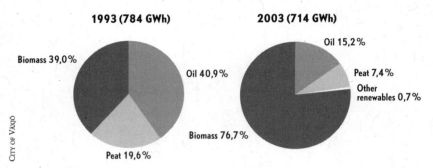

FIGURE 10.1
The City of Växjö increased its sustainable heating from 39% in 1993 to 77% in 2003.[164]

to implement a carbon-free society that are not yet widely available on the market, but carmakers around the world are competing in ramping up their production fast. And advances in nanotechnology, photovoltaics, and sustainable biofuels are continuing to drop the cost of production for these key technologies.

If we add all the initiatives up and implement them in every city, sustainability can be reached even without any state, provincial, or federal help. However, it is clear that support on the state and federal level can greatly accelerate decarbonization. Examples like Canadian and US federal and state support for LEED® buildings (p. 59), Germany's renewable energy (p. 79) and renewable heat energies acts (p. 88), and the UK's zero-carbon home initiative (p. 30) demonstrate how high-level jurisdictional support can make the municipalities' job much easier.

EIGHT SUSTAINABILITY PRINCIPLES

As the preceding chapters have shown, there are a number of strategies that are particularly well suited in moving us closer to sustainability quickly. These are the eight core solutions that allow us to create a carbon-free society — economically and with existing technology — today:

Integrated Design

From buildings to industrial processes to neighborhoods and cities, integrated design is the key. Whole-system analysis does not merely attempt to increase the efficiency of isolated components, but integrates the entire system, eliminating some pieces altogether and maximizing the efficiency of energy and material flows of the whole system instead.

Examples of integrated design include buildings whose building envelope design reduces or eliminates fossil fuel boilers and mechanical ventilation requirements as well as entire neighborhoods that integrate mixed residential and commercial use together with walking, biking, public transit, and cars, rather than relying solely on cars for getting around.

Eco-industrial Design

A related concept, eco-industrial design ensures that one process' waste product becomes another system's feedstock.

Examples include the use of agricultural and forestry waste- and by-products for biofuel output, conversion of household waste into fertilizer, energy, and new products, and the use of sewage for heating, cooling, biofuel, and compost production.

Efficiency

Efficiency is by far the number one source of new, green energy, already outpacing all new oil supplies in the United States. We have been taking advantage of increased efficiency gains per dollar or kWh of output for years, but vast reserves of energy efficiency and energy conservation remain untapped. Efficiency is not the only solution to a carbon-free society, but without efficiency gains, there will be no solution.

Electric and Plug-in Hybrid Cars

Walkable and bikeable communities notwithstanding, efficient electric and plug-in hybrid cars, trucks, and buses in one stroke help solve issues of Peak Oil, national security, and air pollution as well as management of national and international electricity grids powered by renewable energy sources.

Emphasis on Quality of Life

The goal of rational municipal, state, and federal policies cannot be an ever-increasing material and energy consumption, but must instead be ever-increasing health, real wealth, and happiness. A quality of life that can be quantified with community-specific indicators of genuine wealth is ultimately the true indicator of the wealth of a nation (Figures 10.2, 10.3).

Sustainable Biofuels

Oil is running out. Uranium will be running out. The best coal reserves are gone, and the remaining coal represents a huge carbon burden. As an only solution, biofuel would fail because of land requirements. But approached with other solutions such as integrated design, eco-industrial design, and increased efficiency, sustainable biofuels can handily supply all our remaining needs for portable fuels where nothing else makes much sense, for example in air transport, long-distance truck, train, and car hauling, and for peak-demand electrical generation.

Renewable Energy

Renewable Energy is not the first, but the last piece of the puzzle. For most applications, efficiency, integrated design, and eco-industrial design are several orders of magnitude cheaper than renewable energy. However, once all of these

FIGURE 10.2
US data show a pattern of rising real income and a falling index of subjective well-being.[165]

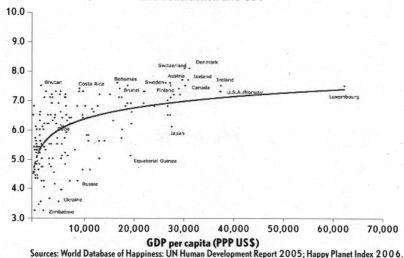

Sources: World Database of Happiness: UN Human Development Report 2005; Happy Planet Index 2006.

FIGURE 10.3
Life satisfaction vs. gross domestic product. Bhutan ranks higher than the US, with a fraction of the income.[166]

options have been exhausted, we still need to get our energy from somewhere. Renewable energy is already more cost-effective or nearly cost-competitive with fossil fuel sources in many cases (good wind sites, remote solar electric installations). Other renewable sources are still expensive (e.g., grid-connected photovoltaics). However, compared to a global economic and environmental collapse, all of these options are cheap. And even the sun and wind alone can meet global energy requirements several times over.

Global Justice

A stable, prosperous, and sustainable planet will only be achieved by universal access to education and political power and when people enjoy minimum levels of economic prosperity. Women rate higher on average in indicators of sustainable behavior, economic sustainability, and prosperity. Societies that, for lack of methane digesters or access to sustainable sources of income, rely on unsustainable fuel-wood harvesting or slash-and-burn agriculture for bare survival endanger global efforts at sustainability. We must provide women with universal access to education, birth control, and political and economic power to accelerate our move to a sustainable world, and we must grant all children of the world access to global education, including internet access, and the chance to participate successfully in the global economy.

THE CARBON FOOTPRINT OF CHANGE

Constructing an infrastructure for wind turbines, more buses, solar panels, plug-in hybrid cars, more building insulation, energy efficient lighting and motors, and all the other requirements for a zero-carbon society is a huge undertaking. Would all that construction activity and demand for concrete, steel, and wood bring about such a large release of greenhouse gases as to send us beyond the tipping point?

The short answer is: no.

Due to relatively low prices for fossil energy in the form of oil, coal, and natural gas in the past, our whole society is built on industrial designs that pay little attention to energy design and compensate by gobbling energy in their operational phase. For example, traditional incandescent light bulbs convert 1.04% or less of primary fossil fuel energy into light. Average cars use less than 0.21% of their energy to move their single-occupancy passenger at city traffic speeds.[167, 168]

Carbon Payback

What is the "embodied energy" — the energy required to make a carbon emission reducing product — compared to its carbon savings? What is the product's energy return on investment (EROI) and what is the measure's carbon return on investment (CROI)? How many years does it take to offset the measure's own manufacturing carbon footprint? In other words, what is the measure's carbon payback?

Carbon Return on Investment

CROI, or the carbon return on investment, indicates how effective each monetary unit (e.g., a dollar) invested is in preventing the emission of additional carbon dioxide into the atmosphere. CROI is the same as CROFI (carbon return on financial investment). Carbon return on carbon investment (CROCI) is the inverse of carbon payback (see text box below).[169]

Carbon payback is the time required for a measure's annual carbon emissions reductions to equal the measure's initial carbon footprint. Carbon payback is usually expressed in years.

Carbon Payback

In financial circles and in energy consultant lingo, payback is the time at which returns equal initial investments. The carbon payback is the point in time at which the carbon emissions generated through introducing a carbon savings measure are equal to the cumulative resulting carbon savings of the measure, compared to baseline emissions.

Energy Payback

Energy payback is the time required for an energy-saving measure's energy savings to equal the initial energy investment. Energy payback is easier to calculate and compare than carbon payback because energy requirements tend to have less regional variation than carbon emissions from energy use. For example, the energy required to heat one pint (about one liter) of water by one degree Celsius at a given temperature and constant air pressure is the same throughout the world. However, the concomitant carbon emissions of energy use vary by energy source and delivery and can range for electricity from about zero pounds per operational kilowatt-hour (kWh) in the case of wind to over 2.2 pounds (1 kg) per kWh in the case of coal.[169]

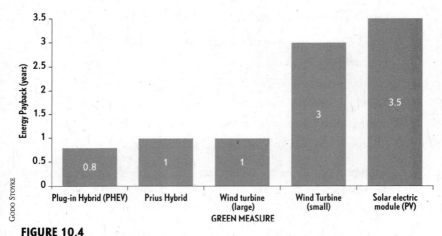

GODO STOYKE

FIGURE 10.4
Approximate energy payback of carbon reduction measures, including green energy and
more efficient cars (lower numbers are better).[102, 125, 169]

Figures 5.4 (p. 73) and 10.4 show the energy payback of a
range of green energy sources. Adjustments for systems analysis
have to be made to reach carbon paybacks. For example, wind turbines often require additional transmission lines for transporting
wind electricity from rural production areas to municipal areas of
consumption. On the other hand, average electricity has much
higher carbon costs than almost all other forms of energy.
Therefore, one kWh of wind electricity offsets far more than one
kWh of the energy used to create and transport the turbine.
Consequently, carbon paybacks are likely to be far better than the
energy payback values indicated. In addition, as society transitions
to a lower carbon economy, carbon gains start a positive feedback
loop, where the embodied energy of carbon reduction measures
shrinks in relation to the percentage of renewable energy used in
the production facility, thereby accelerating the low carbon transi-
tion. Figure 10.4 indicates that the carbon paybacks of the listed
measures are only a few years, or even less than one year in the case
of hybrids or plug-in hybrids. This means that the carbon footprint of change is offset in less than one year in some cases.

THE *NEW* MONTREAL PROTOCOL: PHASE-OUT OF CARBON OVER TEN YEARS

Human-made chlorofluorocarbons (CFCs) were destroying our life-supporting ozone layer — and still will to a lesser extent for another thousand years. The Montreal Protocol on Substances That Deplete the Ozone Layer was a groundbreaking international agreement that opened for signing in 1987. Called by some the most successful international agreement ever signed, it is expected to let our ozone layer recover by 2050.

If we continue with business as usual, or even with half-hearted carbon reduction measures, it is, in light of the world's best science, reasonable to believe that the impact of human-induced increased greenhouse gas levels will ultimately be catastrophic at best or, at worst, result in the extinction of human civilization as

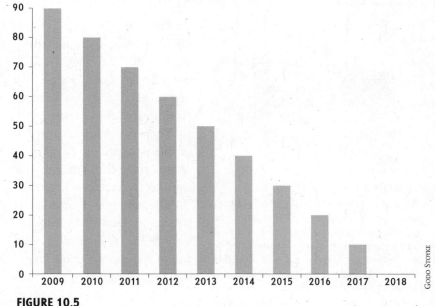

FIGURE 10.5
A phase-out of carbon dioxide and other greenhouse gases over ten years requires an average annual reduction of 10% of current emissions.

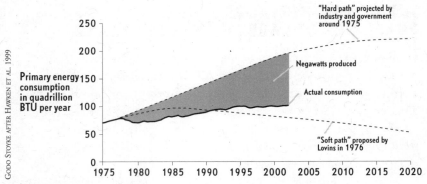

GODO STOYKE AFTER HAWKEN ET AL. 1999

FIGURE 10.6

A comparison of 1975 US industry and government predictions of future energy consumption growth with actual energy developments is a crude approximation of "negawatt production" (saved energy). The declining energy intensity per dollar of gross domestic products is another. Amory Lovins' 1976 proposal of a "soft energy path" based on energy efficiency and renewables turned out to be about four times closer to actual energy consumption levels than the 1975 industry and government projections.[175]

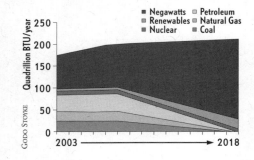

GODO STOYKE

FIGURE 10.7

A proposed path to sustainable energy sources, using the US as an example. It is important to note that energy efficiency and conservation (a watt of saved energy equals a negawatt) are by far the cheapest, greenest and most accessible source of energy. Once the lowest-hanging negawatt fruits have been picked, it is far easier to meet the remaining energy requirements with conventional renewable energy such as wind, solar and biomass.[176]

we know it. Of course, this is not inevitable. If you were driving towards a concrete wall at 60 miles an hour, would you decide to swerve or brake to avoid hitting the obstacle?

There are many reasonable people who believe that we are approaching the carbon-equivalent of a concrete wall fast.

The solution is obvious, if painful (or painfully obvious?): we have to stop emitting CO_2 and other anthropogenic greenhouse gases (GHGs) and ban their net emissions, just as we did with CFCs. I propose a new "Montreal Protocol:" we stop emitting CO_2 and other anthropogenic greenhouse gases (GHGs) and ban their net emissions in the next ten years, by reducing our emissions by 10 % per annum (Figure 10.5). Every year we wait will make the task harder. If we cut 0% in the first year, we will have to cut 11% over the remaining nine years and so on.

These are some of the key steps in achieving a zero carbon society:

- Replace 75-90% of existing energy consumption with efficiency and conservation, using retrofits of existing structures, and better design of new products. (The Rocky Mountain Institute calls a saved watt that replaces a watt of energy produced a "negawatt"; Figure 10.6 shows historic negawatt production, Figure 10.7 includes future negawatt "production" requirements, and Figure 10.8 indicates new negawatt developments required. Overall, negawatts are the cheapest, easiest and greenest source of new energy, and will have to provide the bulk of future energy needs; Figure 10.9.)

- Replace current internal combustion engine (ICE) vehicles with plug-in gas-electric hybrid (PHEV) and full-electric (FE) vehicles.

Historic and proposed future US energy production for the years 2003 to 2018, excluding historic negawatt production

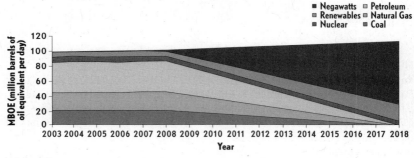

FIGURE 10.8
This sustainable energy path illustrates the negawatts that will have to be created new in addition to historic production (US; historic negawatt production not shown).[176]

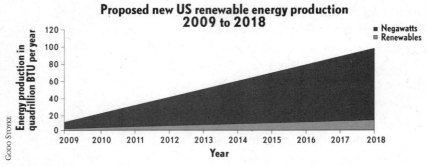

FIGURE 10.9
To achieve a zero carbon society in the next ten years requires the creation of approximately 97 quadrillion BTU of zero emissions (from operations) energy per year by 2018.[176]

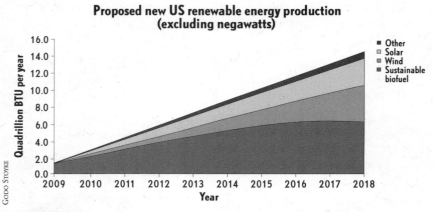

FIGURE 10.10
Proposed new US renewable energy production 2009 to 2018 (excluding negawatts). Even with greatly increased efficiency of energy use, a substantial demand for liquid and solid biofuels will likely remain for some time, as industrial feedstock, for long-distance hauling and flights, and to even out uneven electrical supply from wind and solar (photovoltaics). The role of solar and wind could be greatly increased, and the role of biofuel requirements further decreased, through a greater electrification of our energy economy than assumed, or through the use of hydrogen from renewable sources in combustion engines or fuel cells (current fuel cells are still relatively expensive and heavy, and the efficiency of hydrolysis of water to create hydrogen is not high).[177]

Some key zero carbon challenge metrics for the US: average annual additional production required by 2018[178]

Negawatts produced	2.4 million gigawatt-hours per year
Residential zero carbon/near zero carbon retrofits completed	25.7 billion square feet per year
Commercial zero carbon/near zero carbon retrofits completed	7.2 billion square feet per year
Gas gallon equivalents of biofuel added	7.1 billion gallons
100 Watt photovoltaic modules added	850 million
2 megawatt wind turbines added	18,700

FIGURE 10.11

- Increase efficiency of new light duty vehicles (sedans, vans, SUVs and light pick-up trucks) by a factor of two to ten, depending on vehicle type.

- Move our fossil fuel electrical grid to a 100% renewable one, through a combination of energy efficiency and conservation ("demand-side management" or DSM), wind and solar, smart grids that minimize peak demand through load shifting, long-distance, high voltage DC transmission networks, integration with electric and plug-in hybrid vehicles for renewable electricity storage through V2G ("vehicle-to-grid"), utility-sized electrical storage solutions, and biofuel base load supply to meet solar and wind down-times.

- Convert farming to sustainable ("organic") agriculture that can produce high yields and higher quality food while increasing carbon capture of soils.

- Protect forests and ecosystems through bio-bounties/feebates.

- Meet the reduced remaining building, aviation, electrical and transportation fuel needs through sustainably produced biofuels.

- Move towards a dematerialization of society through emphasis on happiness and quality of life over material consumption, and service and lease models of high quality durable and modular products over disposable consumption.

- Integrate community design to maximize eco-industrial flows of energy and materials, where one waste product becomes the next cycle's feedstock, where walking, biking and public transit take precedence over or get equal consideration with cars, and where the production of food and goods strengthens the local economy.

- Migrate less sustainable industries to more sustainable ones by providing job training and incentives for green switching.

- Keep researching under-utilized renewable energy sources including more efficient products and processes, solar, wind and tides, sustainable biofuel production including algal biodiesel, mycofuels, cellulosic ethanol and biofuel from waste, a hydrogen economy and the climate cooling effect of atmospheric aerosols (p. 14).

NO ORDINARY TIME

The US, at least, has faced a similar problem before.

The year was 1942. The date was January 6th.

US president Franklin Roosevelt held his "State of the Union" address. Less than 30 days before saw the Japanese attack on Pearl Harbour that irrevocably committed a reluctant US into a war with fascist Germany and Imperial Japan. In his address, Roosevelt stunned the nation by outlining the production levels he felt were necessary in 1942 to defeat the axis powers: "Sixty thousand planes, forty-five thousand tanks, twenty thousand anti-aircraft guns, six million tons of merchant shipping." This translated into "a plane every four minutes in 1943; a tank every seven minutes; two seagoing ships a day."

> *Unlike during WWII, we must now bend our will not to join*
> *but to end our undeclared war with nature.*

Roosevelt realized that the car industry was the only industry strong enough to reach this goal. Ironically, both the car and the airplane industry had strongly resisted a conversion previously, the airplane industry on the grounds that the car industry did not have the know-how to build planes, and the car industry on the grounds that they just had one of the best sales years ever and preferred building cars. However, car production was halted, with remaining stocks going to emergency services like police, fire stations, and hospitals, and within nine months US car manufacturing had converted to a powerhouse of production for the military, reaching Roosevelt's goal of 4,000 tanks per month by September of 1942 (Figure 10.6). The production cycle for ships fell from 355 days in 1940 to 194 days in 1941 and 60 days in 1942 (large-scale production of airplanes by the auto industry, however, did take a full 18 months to achieve).

Unlike during WWII, we must now bend our will not to join but to end our undeclared war with nature. Instead of tanks, bombers, and naval ships, we need to redesign our products and cities, build massive numbers of plug-in hybrids and huge numbers of wind turbines and solar installations, make every effort to redirect agricultural and forestry waste and household sewage to sustainable biofuel, and begin a building retrofit program unparalleled in the history of humankind.

Just as in any other time of change, there will be strenuous opposition by some on the grounds of personal gain, ideology, ignorance, or a simple unwillingness to change. However, despite strong efforts by a few at distortion, the science is clear: this is an effort that can and must be undertaken. We have the technology and the

HEMERA TECHNOLOGIES INC.

means to make this effort. Roosevelt's 1942 State of the Union address provides a fitting concluding remark:

"Let no man [or woman] say that it cannot be done."[172]

MORE INFO

- The mother lode on climate change — the latest report of the Intergovernmental Panel on Climate Change (IPCC): ipcc.ch/ipccreports/ar4-wg1.htm.
- Questions on climate change answered in plain English: real climate.org
- "Climate change: A guide for the perplexed" from *NewScientist*: newscientist.com/article/dn11462
- Information on the backgrounds of climate deniers and climate sceptics, their often false credentials and funding sources: desmog blog.com.
- Tips for assessing the quality of information on climate change: newscientist.com/article/dn11637.

Super Grid (HVDC)

- European high-voltage direct current cables for distribution of renewable energy:
- radionetherlands.nl/development/090305-super-grid

Books:

- Lester R. Brown. 2008. *Plan B 3.0: Mobilizing to Save Civilization.* W.W. Norton.
- Guy Dauncey. (September 2009). *The Great Climate Challenge — 101 Solutions for a Post-Carbon World.* New Society Publishers.
- Thomas L. Friedman. 2008. *Hot, Flat and Crowded.* Farrar, Straus and Giroux.

QuickLink: CarbonCharter.org/28

CARBON CHARTER
COMPANION WEBSITE

Visit the Carbon Charter companion website at
CarbonCharter.org

The site contains:

- updates of sustainability bylaws
- added material that didn't fit into this book
- links to original source material
- readers' feedback and contributions

See you at the site!

RESOURCES

To quickly access links to information presented in this book, please visit the companion website at **carboncharter.org**

Sustainability Organizations with Municipal Members

Global

ICLEI — Local Governments for Sustainability: iclei.org

ICLEI was founded in 1990 as the "International Council for Local Environmental Initiatives." The Council was established when more than 200 local governments from 43 countries convened at a conference, the World Congress of Local Governments for a Sustainable Future, at the United Nations in New York. [173] The organization is aimed at municipalities from around the world that are working towards sustainability. Also see the World Mayors Council on Climate Change at iclei.org/index. php?id=7192

C40 Cities: c40cities.org. Efforts by 40 of the world's largest cities to tackle climate change.

US

Mayors Climate Protection Center of the United States Conference of Mayors: usmayors.org/climateprotection

The members of the Conference consist of American cities with a population of 30,000 or more, including 1,139 such cities in 2007.

Cool Counties Climate Stabilization Declaration: kingcounty.gov/exec/coolcounties.aspx

An initiative led by King County, Washington, Fairfax County, Virginia, and Nassau County, New York, in association with the Sierra Club, committing to 80% reductions in carbon emissions by 2050 and calling for increased federal fuel standards.

Canada

The Federation of Canadian Municipalities (fcm.ca) operates sustainable communities programs at sustainable communities.fcm.ca

See, for example, the Partners for Climate Protection program at sustainablecommunities.fcm.ca/files/Capacity_Building_-_PCP/pcp-overview-En.pdf

Europe

Climate Alliance/Alianza del Clima e.V.: klimabuendnis.org/

The largest European city network for climate protection with over 1,200 city, town, and county members. Sites are available in English (climatealliance.org), German (klimabuendnis.org), Spanish (klimabuendnis.org), Italian (climatealliance.it/public/), Dutch (klimaatverbond.nl), and for Luxembourg (oeko.lu//index.php?idusergroup=5).

DENISE DAHL

125

Energie-Cités, the Association of European local authorities promoting local sustainable energy policy: energie-cites.org This is a coalition of over 1,000 cities and towns in 30 countries promoting sustainable energy use.

Other Organizations Promoting Municipal Sustainability

Sustainable Land Development International (SLDI): sldi.org An industry group that provides sustainable development information for land developers and other interested parties. Publishes two free sustainable development online magazines:
Sustainable Land Development Today: sldtonline.com
Online sustainable urban redevelopment magazine: surmag.com
Conferences organized by SLDI:
Land Development Breakthroughs: Best Practices Conferences and Workshops, available at ldbreak throughs.com (e.g., workshops on biomass, pervious concrete, site soil management)
Sustainable development bookstore: sldi.org/index.php?option= com_content&task=view&id=50& Itemid=64

QuickLink: carboncharter.org/29

Online Information Resources

Post Carbon Cities: Preparing local governments for energy and climate uncertainty, at postcarboncities.net/ This is a comprehensive website of municipal initiatives by the Post Carbon Institute.
State of Massachusetts link to free Smart Growth and Sustainable Development principles: commpres.env.state. ma.us/content/publications.asp
The City Fix: website with articles on sustainability for cities at thecity fix.com
Sierra Club Cool Cities: coolcities.us

Books

Climate Protection Manual for Cities from Rocky Mountain Institute cofounder Hunter Lovins' non-profit organization Natural Capitalism Solutions (natcapsolutions.org) describes how to create a municipal climate action plan.
For information about the book, see natcapsolutions.org/ClimatePro tectionManual.htm
Free at climatemanual.org/Cities/ downloads/ClimateProtectionMan ual_Cities.pdf
Fill out the survey at climatemanual. org/Cities/index.htm
A Pattern Language: Towns, Buildings, Construction. This 1977 timeless classic by Christopher Alexander and several co-authors has lost none of its relevance in the last 30 years. Brilliant analysis of energy flows and human needs from the micro- to the macro-scale.

QuickLink: CarbonCharter.org/30

BEN ORKAAN – STOCKXCHNG

ENDNOTES

1. United Nations. 2008. "The Millennium Development Goals Report: 2008." Available at mdgs.un.org/unsd/mdg/Resources/Static/Products/Progress 2008 /MDG_Report_2008_En.pdf

2. United Nations. September 11, 2008. Millennium Development Goals Indicators. Retrieved October 4, 2008, from mdgs.un.org/unsd/mdg/Default.aspx

3. Worldwatch Institute. 2008. *2008 State of the World: Innovations for a Sustainable Economy*. W.W. Norton.

4. United Nations. 2008. "The Millennium Development Goals Report: 2008 Addendum." Available at mdgs.un.org/unsd/mdg/Resources/Static/Products/Progress2008/MDG_Report_2008_Addendum_En.pdf

5. UNICEF. 2007. "MDG 7: Ensure environmental sustainability — Safe drinking water." Retrieved December 21, 2008, from unicef.org/progressforchildren/2007n6/index_41841.htm

6. Matthew Cimitile. 2008. "Mangroves: Tampa Bay's Cash Crop?" *BaySoundings*. Retrieved December 20, 2008, from baysoundings.com/Stories/feature.asp

7. Island Press. 2007. "Millennium Ecosystem Assessment: A Toolkit for Understanding and Action." Available from islandpress.org/assets/library/27_matoolkit.pdf

8. Wikipedia. August 24, 2008. "Millennium Ecosystem Assessment." Retrieved September 23, 2008, from en.wikipedia.org/wiki/Millennium_Ecosystem_Assessment

9. Millennium Ecosystem Assessment Board. 2005. "Living Beyond our Means: Natural Assets and Human Well-being." Millennium Ecosystem Assessment. Retrieved June 25, 2008, from millenniumassessment.org/documents/document.429.aspx.pdf

10. Kirsten Garrett. January 28, 2001. "Natural Capitalism: A lecture by Amory Lovins." Radio National. Retrieved September 23, 2008, from abc.net.au/rn/talks/bbing/stories/s231834.htm

11. Robert Costanza et al. 1997. "The value of the world's ecosystem services and natural capital." *Nature* 387: 253–60.

12. World Wildlife Fund, UNEP World Conservation Monitoring Centre, and Global Footprint Network (eds.). 2004. *Living Planet Report 2004*. Banson Production.

13. International Union for Conservation of Nature (IUCN). 2008. "About IUCN." Retrieved October 4, 2008, from iucn.org/about/index.cfm.

14. International Union for Conservation of Nature (IUCN). 2008. "The IUCN Red List of Threatened Species 2008." Retrieved October 4, 2008, from iucn.org/about/work/programmes/species/red_list/index.cfm Link expired. See also iucnredlist.org/

15. Science Daily. 2008. "House mouse: Mus musculus is the common house mouse." Retrieved October 5, 2008, from sciencedaily.com/articles/h/house_mouse.htm

16. Intergovernmental Panel on Climate Change (IPCC). 2007. *Contribution of Working Group I to the*

127

Fourth Assessment Report of the IPCC. Climate Change 2007 — The Physical Science Basis. Cambridge University Press: 4: SPM.2. Available free from ipcc.ch/ipccreports/ar4-wg1.htm

17. Wikipedia. September 28, 2008. "List of Kyoto Protocol signatories." Retrieved October 5, 2008, from en.wikipedia.org/wiki/List_of_Kyoto_Protocol_signatories

18. Colin J. Campbell and Jean H. Laherrère. 1998. "The End of Cheap Oil: Global production of conventional oil will begin to decline sooner than most people think, probably within 10 years." *Scientific American*, March 1998: 78–83. Retrieved November 2, 2008, from dieoff.org/page140.pdf (formatting differs slightly from *Scientific American* version).

19. US Government Energy Information Administration. July 28, 2008. "Annual U.S. Crude Oil Field Production [1859–2007]." Retrieved November 2, 2008, from tonto.eia.doe.gov/dnav/pet/hist/mcrfpus2a.htm

20. US Government Energy Information Administration. July 28, 2008. "U.S. Crude Oil Field Production (Thousand Barrels per Day) [1900–2007]." Retrieved November 2, 2008, from tonto.eia.doe.gov/dnav/pet/hist_xls/MCRFPUS2a.xls

21. Wikipedia. October 1, 2008. "M. King Hubbert." Retrieved November 2, 2008, from en.wikipedia.org/wiki/M._King_Hubbert

22. Cutler J. Cleveland et al. 1984. "Energy and the U.S. Economy: A Biophysical Perspective." *Science*, 225 (4665): 890–7.

23. Joel K. Bourne and Robert Clark. 2007. "Green Dreams." *National Geographic*, October 2007: 38–59. Available at ngm.nationalgeographic.com/2007/10/biofuels/biofuels-text

24. Charles Hall. 2008. "Unconventional Oil: Tar Sands and Shale Oil — EROI on the Web, Part 3 of 6." Retrieved December 10, 2008, from theoildrum.com/node/3839 EROI calculations for tar sands range from 1.5 to 7.2.

25. Lee R. Lynd et al. 2007. "Energy Myth Three: High Land Requirements and an Unfavourable Energy Balance Preclude Biomass Ethanol from Playing a Large Role in Providing Energy Services." In: Benjamin K. Sovacool and Marilyn A. Brown (eds.). *Energy and American Society: Thirteen Myths.* Springer, 75–101.

26. David Blume. 2007. *Alcohol Can Be a Gas! Fueling an Ethanol Revolution for the 21st Century.* International Institute for Ecological Agriculture.

27. US Government Energy Information Administration. August 24, 2008. "Long-Term World Oil Supply: A Resource Base/Production Path Analysis." Retrieved November 2, 2008, from eia.doe.gov/emeu/plugs/plworld.html

28. US Government Energy Information Administration. October 23, 2008. "World Production of Crude Oil, NGPL, and Other Liquids, and Refinery Processing Gain, Most Recent Annual Estimates, 1980-2007." Retrieved November 2, 2008, from eia.doe.gov/emeu/international/RecentTotalOilSupplyBarrelsperDay.xls

29. Association for the Study of Peak Oil (ASPO) – USA. 2008. "Worldwide Oil Production." Retrieved December 22, 2008, from aspousa.org

30. Ana Monteiro and Scott Marx (eds.). 2007. "Peak Oil Task Force/City and County of San Francisco: Background Documents." City and County of San Francisco. Available at sfenvironment.org/downloads/library/peakoilbackgrounder.pdf

31. Bruce Robinson. 2004. "London's Burning: The Great Fire." BBC. Retrieved November 3, 2008, from bbc.co.uk/history/british/civil_war_revolution/great_fire_01.shtml

32. Anniina Jokinen. 2007. "The Great Fire of London, 1666." *Luminarium.* Retrieved November 3, 2008, from luminarium.org/encyclopedia/greatfire.htm

33. Wikipedia. October 28, 2008. "Great Fire of London." Retrieved November 3, 2008, from en.wikipedia.org/wiki/Great_Fire_of_London

34. Channel 4. 2008. "Legacy of the Fire." Retrieved November 3, 2008, from channel4.com/history/microsites/H/history/fire/legacy.html

35. Roy D. Adler. 2002. "Women in the Executive Suite Correlate to Higher Profits." *European Project on Equal Pay.* Retrieved December 13, 2008, from equalpay.nu/docs/en/adler_web.pdf

36. Del Jones. December 30, 2003. "2003: Year of the woman among the 'Fortune' 500?" *USA Today.* Retrieved December 13, 2008, from usatoday.com/money/companies/management/2003-12-30-womenceos_x.htm This study found that the eight Fortune 500 companies led by women in 2003 outperformed their male-led Fortune 500 counterparts financially by 25% (52% gain vs. 27% gain on the S & P 500 index).

37. Rafael Brusilow. April 7, 2008. "Is it a woman's corporate world?" *Metro,* 10. A corporate research study by NGO Catalyst found that in 2007 Fortune 500 companies with the highest percentages of women on the board performed 42% to 66% better than those with lower representation.

38. Some oppose quotas on the grounds that hiring should be based

strictly on merit. However, this position assumes that current hiring practices are merit-based. An unintentional experiment from the music world suggests otherwise. The data comes from a study by Cecilia Rouse, associate professor in Princeton's Woodrow Wilson School of Public and International Affairs and the Economics Department, and Claudia Goldin, a professor of economics at Harvard University. Until the 1970s, female representation in orchestras was around 10%. According to an article in the *Princeton Weekly Bulletin,* "[r]enowned conductors have asserted that female musicians have 'smaller technique', are more temperamental and are simply unsuitable for orchestras, and some European orchestras do not hire women at all." However, it had been difficult to prove discrimination in hiring processes. In the 1970s and 1980s, most major US orchestras began to democratize hiring by advertising positions, allowing orchestra members to participate in hiring, and introducing an interview system that eliminated face-to-face interviews in favor of screened application ("blind auditions") that prevented biases on the basis of gender or other grounds. Instead, initial screening for hiring was based entirely on the applicant's ability to perform musically. It turned out that eliminating visual cues as to the applicant's identity was insufficient, as some hiring committees would listen to the footsteps of the applicants, often distinguishing male shoes from female high heels. So the next step was the introduction of carpets in interview rooms to eliminate this factor as well. The study compared blind and non-blind auditions. While non-blind auditions favored men, advancing only 46.2% of women, blind auditions favored women, advancing 58.6% to the next round. Though final selection was usually still not blind, overall, the study found that blind auditions increased the chance of a woman's selection by 50%, increasing female representation to about 35% in the mid-1990s. Marilyn Marks. February 12, 2001. "Blind auditions key to hiring musicians. *Princeton Weekly Bulletin.* Retrieved July 11, 2008, from princeton.edu/pr/pwb/01/0212/7b.shtml

39. Christine Toomey. June 8, 2008. "Quotas for women on the board: do they work? *Times Online.* Retrieved November 6, 2008, from women.timesonline.co.uk/tol/life_and_style/women/article4066740.ece

40. Christoph Seidler. September 25, 2008. "Gefährliches Methanhydrat: Klimakiller löst sich aus den Tiefen des Eismeeres." *Spiegel Online.* Retrieved September 29, 2008, from spiegel.de/wissenschaft/natur/0,1518,580213,00.html

41. Christine Dell'Amore. July 22, 2008. "Arctic Dispatch: A Thaw in the Arctic Tundra." *Smithsonian.* Retrieved September 29, 2008, from smithsonianmag.com/science-nature/arctic-dispatch-10.html

42. James Hansen. 2008. "Clock running out on irreversible climate change: Part I." Retrieved September 29, 2008, from sciencealert.com.au/opinions/20081505-17325.html

43. Asgeir Sorteberg. 2008. "Arctic sea ice loss compared to IPCC projections." Retrieved January 7, 2009, from carbonequity.info/images/seaice 07.jpg

44. It must be noted that, strictly speaking, "zero-carbon" and "fossil-fuel free" do not necessarily mean the same thing as "zero greenhouse gases" since the latter include methane, stratospheric ozone, sulfur hexafluoride, nitrous oxide, and halocarbons, including CFCs. However, carbon dioxide is responsible for the bulk of anthropogenic climate change and is therefore highlighted here for stylistic simplicity. By the same token, "zero-carbon" obviously refers to "net-zero emissions of carbon dioxide from human activity," as carbon is a basic building block of nature.

45. Tom Young. November 5, 2008. "Climate change to take formal role in planning decisions." *Business Green.* Retrieved November 26, 2008, from businessgreen.com/business-green/news/2229836/national

46. Göran Persson. 2006. "Enduring Freedom?: Sweden's plans to wean itself off oil. *Renewable Energy World,* September–October 2006: 157–61.

47. Bundesministerium für Umwelt, Naturschutz und Reaktorsicherheit. 2007. *Begründung: A. Allgemeines.* Bundesministerium für Umwelt, Naturschutz und Reaktorsicherheit. Available at bmu.de/files/pdfs/allgemein/application/pdf/entwurf_ee_recht_begra.pdf Link expired.

48. Stephen Leahy. June 24, 2008. "Straightgoods.ca: Simple measures can cut carbon emissions." *United Nations Environment Programme: The Environment in the News,* June 26, 2008. Available at unep.org/cpi/briefs/2008June26.doc

49. Växjö kommun. 2007. "Fossil Fuel Free Växjö." Retrieved December 14, 2007, from vaxjo.se/vaxjo_templates/Page.aspx?id=1664

50. Wikipedia. September 24, 2008. "Växjö." Retrieved September 29, 2008, from en.wikipedia.org/wiki/Växjö

51. World Clean Energy Awards. 2007. "Nominee: City of Vaxjo, Sweden." Retrieved September 29, 2008, from cleanenergyawards.com/top-navigation/nominees-projects/nominee-detail/project/29/

52. Bo Frank. No date. "Fossil Fuel Free: Växjö Sweden." Växjö kommun. Retrieved September 29, 2008, from

energiecites.eu/IMG/pdf/imagine_session4_ppt_frank_en.pdf

53. Växjö kommun. No date. "Climate Strategy of Växjö." Växjö kommun. Retrieved December 14, 2007, from vaxjo.se/vaxjo_templates/Page.aspx?id=1664

54. Växjö kommun. 2008. "Sustainable Development." Växjö kommun. Retrieved December 14, 2007, from vaxjo.se/vaxjo_templates/Page.aspx?id=1661

55. Växjö kommun. 2008. "Decoupling." Växjö kommun. Available at vaxjo.se/vaxjo_templates/Page.aspx?id=1661

56. Energie-Cités. 2003. "A Fossil Fuel Free Växjö." Retrieved September 29, 2008, from energie-cites.eu/IMG/pdf/cf05_wg2_hellstrom.pdf

57. Växjö kommun. 2007. "Fossil Fuel Free Växjö." Växjö kommun. Available at vaxjo.se/upload/3880/CO2%20engelska%202007.pdf

58. Wikipedia. September 18, 2008. "Carbon Footprint." Retrieved September 20, 2008, from en.wikipedia.org/wiki/Carbon_footprint

59. BSI British Standards. 2008. "PAS 2050: Assessing the life cycle greenhouse gas emissions of goods and services." Retrieved September 20, 2007, from bsi-global.com/en/ Standards -and-Publications/How-we-can-help-you/Professional-Standards-Service/PAS-2050/

60. BSI British Standards. 2008. "BS EN ISO 14040: 2006 — Environmental management. Life cycle assessment. Principles and framework." Retrieved September 20, 2007, from bsigroup.com/en/Shop/Publication-Detail/?pid=000000000030154435

61. BSI British Standards. 2008. "BS EN ISO 14044: 2006 — Environ-mental management. Life cycle assessment. Requirements and guidelines." Retrieved September 20, 2007, from bsigroup.com/en/Shop/Publication-Detail/?pid=000000000030154427

62. Food, Nutrition & Science. November 26, 2007. "Carbon Footprint Food Labels." Retrieved September 21, 2008, from food nutrition science.com/index.cfm/do/monsanto.ar ticle/articleId/91.cfm

63. Matthew Sparkes. May 31, 2007. "Carbon Footprint Labels for UK Produce." *Treehugger*. Retrieved September 21, 2008, from treehugger.com/files/2007/05/carbon_footprin.php

64. Tania Branigan and Helen Carter. May 31, 2007. "Carbon labels to help shoppers save planet." *Guardian*. Retrieved September 21, 2008, from guardian.co.uk/environment/2007/may/31/greenpolitics.retail

65. Karen Charlesworth. August 22, 2008. "Counting the cost of carbon." *PrintWeek*. Retrieved September 20, 2008, from printweek.com/business/news/840489/Counting-cost-carbon/

66. Ian Herbert. March 16, 2007. "Carbon footprint of products to be displayed on label package." *The Independent.* Retrieved September 22, 2008, from independent.co.uk/environment/climate-change/carbon-footprint-of-products-to-be-displayed-on-label-package-440447.html

67. Walkers. 2007. "Walkers carbon footprint." Retrieved October 6, 2008, from walkerscarbonfootprint.co.uk/walkers _carbon_footprint.html

68. Dominique Patton. April 29, 2008. "Tesco carbon footprint labels back organic, says Soil Association." *Food Navigator.* Retrieved September 22, 2008, from foodnavigator.com/Financial-Industry /Tesco-carbon-footprint-labels-back-organic-says-Soil-Association

69. Japan Ministry of Economy, Trade and Industry. July 31, 2008. "The first meeting of the Domestic Committee for International Standardization of the Carbon Footprint System." Retrieved September 22, 2008, from meti. go.jp/english/press/data/nBackIssue2008073 1_03.html

70. Japan Probe. September 11, 2008. "Sapporo Breweries to put carbon footprints on product labels." Retrieved September 21, 2008, from japanprobe.com/?p=6126

71. Bill Belew. September 19, 2008. "Carbon Footprint on Beer Labels in Japan." *Greenpacks*. Retrieved September 22, 2008, from greenpacks.org/2008/09/19/carbon-footprint-on-beer-labels-in-japan/

72. Rainer Griesshammer. 2008. "Carbon footprinting for a better climate? Retailers and manufacturers are working on CO₂ product labelling." *eco@work*, January 2008: 12-13. Retrieved January 24, 2008, from oeko.de/files/e-paper-eng/080122/application/ pdf/e081_epaper.pdf

73. City of Seattle, Office of the Mayor. February 16, 2005. "Mayor calls for Seattle, other cities to meet protocol goals." Retrieved October 5, 2008, from seattle.gov/mayor/newsdetail.asp?ID=4973&dept=40

74. Tom Cochran. April 2, 2007. "Statement of the United States Conference of Mayors Executive Director Tom Cochran on Supreme Court Decision on EPA Control over Emissions." The United States Conference of Mayors. Available at usmayors.org/climateprotection/supremecourtEPA_040207.pdf

75. The United States Conference of Mayors. 2008. "Mayors Climate Protection Center." Retrieved October 5, 2008, from usmayors.org

76. The United States Conference of Mayors. 2007. "U.S. Conference of Mayors Climate Protection Agreement." Retrieved October 5, 2008, from usmayors.org/climateprotection/agree ment.htm

77. European Commission. 2008. "Covenant of Mayors." Retrieved September 27, 2008, from sustenergy. org/tpl/page.cfm?pageName=covenant_of_mayors2

78. William D. Nordhaus and James Tobin. 1973. "Is Growth Obsolete?" In: Milton Moss (ed.), *The Measurement of Economic and Social Performance.* National Bureau of Economic Research. Available at cowles.econ.yale.edu/P/cp/p03b/p0398a.pdf

79. Gernot Wagner. 2007. "Green Accounting." Retrieved November 5, 2008, from gwagner.com/research/green_accounting

80. Jane Qiu. August 2, 2007. "Special report: China's green accounting system on shaky ground. *Nature*, 448: 518–9.

81. National Research Council. 1999. *Nature's Numbers: Expanding the National Economic Accounts to Include the Environment.* National Academies Press.

82. Gernot Wagner. 2001. "U.S. Timber Accounts, 1957–1997." Available at gwagner.com/writing/011009 US_Timber_Accounts.pdf

83. United Nations, European Commission, International Monetary Fund, Organisation for Economic Co-operation, and World Bank. 2003. "Handbook of National Accounting: Integrated Environmental and Economic Accounting 2003." Available at unstats.un.org/unsd/envAccounting/seea2003.pdf

84. UK Office for National Statistics. 2008. "Environmental Accounts: Spring 2008." UK Office for National Statistics. Available at statistics. gov.uk/downloads/theme_environment/EA_Jun08.pdf

85. Redefining Progress. 2008. "Genuine Progress Indicator." Retrieved November 5, 2008, from rprogress.org/sustainability_indicators/genuine_progress_indicator.htm.

86. Wikipedia. October 15, 2008. "Genuine Progress Indicator." Retrieved November 5, 2008, from en.wikipedia.org/wiki/Genuine_Progress_Indicator

87. Mark Winfield et al. 2007. "Ontario Community Sustainability Report — 2007." Pembina Institute. Available at pubs.pembina.org/reports/ocsr-07-report.pdf

88. Mark Anielski and Jeff Wilson. May 15, 2006. "City of Leduc 2005 Genuine Well-being Report." *Anielski Management.* Available at leduc.ca/Leduc/1024/News_and_Events/initiatives/gwa.asp

89. Lucy Siegle. March 23, 2008. "This much I know: Amory Lovins." *Guardian.* Retrieved September 24, 2008, from guardian.co.uk/environment/2008/mar/23/ethicalliving.lifeandhealth4

90. Amory B. Lovins et al. 2004. "Winning the Oil Endgame: Innovation for Profits, Jobs and Security." Rocky Mountain Institute. Available for free (with registration) at oilendgame.com

91. UK Government. 2008. "Energy Performance Certificate." Retrieved September 27, 2008, from direct.gov.uk/en/HomeAndCommunity/BuyingAndSellingYourHome/Homeinformationpacks/DG_076370

92. European Commission, Directorate-General for Energy and Transport. 2008. "Implementation of the European Performance of Buildings Directive: Country Reports." Available at buildingsplatform.eu/epbd_publication/doc/EPBD_BuPLa_Country%20reports_20080624_2_p3126.pdf

93. European Parliament. January 4, 2003. "Directive 2002/91/EC of the European Parliament and of the Council of 16 December 2002 on the energy performance of buildings." *Official Journal of the European Communities,* L 1/65–71. Available at eurlex.europa.eu/LexUriServ/LexUriServ.do?uri=OJ:L:2003:001:0065:0071:EN:PDF

94. UK Government. 2008. "Energy Performance of Buildings: Overview." Retrieved September 27, 2008, from communities.gov.uk/planningandbuilding/theenvironment/energyperformance/overview/

95. European Commission, Directorate-General for Energy and Transport. 2006. "EPBD Building Platform — FAQ: Certification procedures." Retrieved September 27, 2008, from buildingsplatform.org/cms/index.php?id=93

96. UK Government. 2008. "What is an Energy Performance Certificate?" Retrieved September 27, 2008, from direct.gov.uk/en/Home And Community/BuyingAndSellingYour Home/Homeinformationpacks/DG_076370.

97. UK Government. 2008. "Home Condition Report: Sample." Available at homeinformation packs.gov.uk/pdf/sampleHCR.pdf

98. UK Government. 2008. "Energy Performance Certificate [Sample]." Available at communities.gov.uk/documents/planningandbuilding/pdf/319282.pdf

99. Wikipedia. September 26, 2008. "Energy Performance Certificate." Retrieved September 27, 2008, from en.wikipedia.org/wiki/Energy_Performance_Certificate

100. Wikipedia. September 22, 2008. "Energy Performance Certificate."

Retrieved September 27, 2008, from en.wikipedia.org/wiki/Energy_efficiency _in_British_housing

101. US Environmental Protection Agency. 2008. "Features of ENERGY STAR Qualified New Homes." US Environmental Protection Agency. Retrieved September 27, 2008, from energystar.gov/index.cfm?c= new_homes.nh_features

102. Carbon Busters Inc. calculations, December 19, 2008.

103. Building orientation is described for northern hemisphere locations. Please note that if you live in the southern hemisphere, you have to replace all references to "south" and "southern" with "north" and "northern" to maximize building efficiency.

104. City of Bend. 2008. "Bend Code 10–10.26A." Retrieved November 5, 2008, from ci.bend.or.us/depts/com munity_development/planning_division

105. Kurt Newick and Andy Black. 2005. "California's Solar Access Laws." Retrieved August 19, 2008, from solar depot.com/pdf/CASolarAccessLaws. pdf.

106. International Code Council. March 5, 2007. "ICC Green Building White Paper." Retrieved November 4, 2008, from iccsafe.org/news/ green/pdf/ ICC_Green_Building_White_Paper. pdf

107. Daniel Lerch. 2007. *Post Carbon Cities: Planning for Energy and Climate Uncertainty*. Post Carbon Press.

108. Walkable Communities. 2008. "Frequently Asked Questions." Walkable Communities. Retrieved December 9, 2008, from walkable. org/ faqs.html.

109. Yoriko Kishimoto. March 19, 2007. "2007 State of the City Address." Retrieved December 8, 2008, from city ofpaloalto.org/civica/filebank/blobdload .asp?BlobID=11031

110. Andreas Wetz. September 8, 2008. "Verkehr: So wird Österreich zum Fahrrad-Land." *Die Presse*. Retrieved September 9, 2008, from diepresse. com/home/panorama/oesterreich/ 412608/index.do?_vl_backlink=/home/ index.do

111. Michael Meschik. 2008. *Planungshandbuch Radverkehr*. Springer.

112. Dave Olsen. July 9, 2007. "No Hassle Transit?: Try Hasselt." Retrieved January 7, 2009, from thetye. ca/Views/2007/07/09/NoFares3/

113. Wikipedia. November 1, 2008. "Public transport in Hasselt." Retrieved November 6, 2008, from en.wikipedia.org/wiki/Public_transport _in_Hasselt

114. Wikipedia. November 4, 2008. "Hasselt." Retrieved November 6, 2008, from en.wikipedia.org/wiki/ Hasselt

115. Elisabeth Wehrmann. 1997. "Stadt ohne Fahrschein." *Zeit Online*, 48/1997. Retrieved November 6, 2008, from zeit.de/1997/48/Stadt_ohne_ Fahrschein?page=all

116. Claudia Zimmermann. July 30, 2007. "Magnet für die Region." Westdeutscher Rundfunk. Available at zukunft-ennstal.at/pdfs/HASSELT.pdf

117. City of Hasselt. 2008. "Hauptstadt des guten Geschmacks." Retrieved November 7, 2008, from hasselt.be/content/content/record.php ?ID=4417 Link expired.

118. Ruth Reichstein. August 24, 2008. "Wo der Bus gratis ist." Retrieved November 6, 2008, from ortszeit.org/ ?p=550

119. Zukunftswerkstatt. November 14, 2007. "Vorteil Hasselt — kostenloser Nahverkehr." Retrieved November 6, 2008, from www.zukunfts werkstatton-line.de/doc/hasselt.pdf

120. Carbon Busters Inc. calculations, December 14, 2008.

121. Jeff Tollefson. 2008. "Charging up the Future." *Nature* 456: 436–40. Full article available (for a fee) from nature.com/news/2008/081126/full/456436a.html

122. Sherry Boschert. 2006. *Plug-in Hybrids: The Cars That Will Recharge America*. New Society Publishers.

123. Carbon Busters Inc. calculations, November 6, 2008.

124. John Lettice. March 27, 2008. "A Double Deck of Green ..." *The Register*. Retrieved Dec. 14, 2008, from theregister.co.uk/2008/03/27/denmark_agassi_ev/

125. Heather L. Maclean and Lester B. Lave. 1988. "A Life-Cycle Model of an Automobile." *Environmental Policy Analysis*, 3: 322A–30A. Summary at Institute for Lifecycle Environmental Assessment. September 12, 2003. "Automobiles: Manufacture vs. Use." Retrieved June 19, 2006, from iere.org/ILEA/lcas/macleanlave1998.html

126. CalCars. July 19, 2007. "EPRI-NRDC Definitive Study: PHEVs Will Reduce Emissions If Broadly Adopted." *CalCars*. Retrieved November 27, 2008, from calcars.org/calcars-news/797.html The full report is available at my.epri.com/portal/server.pt?open=512&objID=243&PageID=223132&cached=true&mode=2

127. Stephen D. Solomon. 2008. "For Security, Get Off Oil: Former CIA director R. James Woolsey says America's oil dependence is a grave threat." *Scientific American Earth 3.0*, September 2008: 50–3. Retrieved January 7, 2009, from ciam.com/ article .cfm?id=is-oil-a-threat

128. Austin Energy. 2008. "Plug-in Austin: Building a Market for Gas-Optional Hybrids." Retrieved November 6, 2008, from austinenergy.com/About%20Us/Environmental%20Initiatives/Plug-in%20Hybrid%20Vehicles/index.htm

129. Austin Energy. 2008. "Creating a Market for PHEVs in Austin: Making PHEVs Attractive." Retrieved November 6, 2008, from austinenergy.com/About%20Us/Environmental%20Initiatives/Plug-in%20Hybrid%20Vehicles/creatingMarketInAustin.htm

130. Roger Duncan and Michael J. Osborne. 2005. "Report on Transportation Convergence." Available at pluginpartners.org/includes/pdfs/gasOptionalvehicles.pdf

131. Transport for London. 2008. "Blue Badge holders." Retrieved May 16, 2008, from tfl.gov.uk/roadusers/congestioncharging/6736.aspx

132. Wikipedia. May 14, 2008. "London congestion charge." Retrieved May 16, 2008, from en.wikipedia.org/wiki/London_congestion_charge

133. Wikipedia, September 1, 2008. "Stockholm congestion tax." Retrieved September 4, 2008, from en.wikipedia.org/wiki/Stockholm_congestion_tax

134. UK Government. May 15, 2006. "Road Charging Scheme: Europe–Italy, Rome." Available from cfit.gov.uk/map/pdf/europe-italy-rome.pdf

135. Government of Malta. 2007. "CVA System: The Purpose Of." Retrieved December 2, 2008, from cva.gov.mt

136. Wikipedia. September 8, 2008. "Erneuerbare-Energien-Gesetz." Retrieved September 10, 2008, from de.wikipedia.org/wiki/Erneuerbare-Energien-Gesetz

137. Fraunhofer Institute and Energy Economics Group. 2005. *Feed-In Systems in Germany and Spain and a comparison*. Retrieved September 10, 2008, from erneuerbareenergien.de/files/english/renewable_energy/downloads/application/pdf/langfassung_einspeise systeme_en.pdf

138. Eric Reguly. March 21, 2008. "Lessons from Germany's Energy Renaissance." *Globe and Mail*. Retrieved May 9, 2008, from forum.skyscraper page.com/archive/index.php/t-148 020.html

139. Bundesministerium für Umwelt, Naturschutz und Reaktorsicherheit. 2007. "EEG-Erfahrungsbericht 2007 zum Erneuerbare-Energien-Gesetz (EEG-Erfahrungsbericht)." Available at bmu. de/files/pdfs/allgemein/application/pdf/erfahrungsbericht_eeg_2007_zf.pdf

140. Bundesministerium für Umwelt, Naturschutz und Reaktorsicherheit. 2008. *Atomkraft — ein teurer Irrweg: Die Mythen der Atomwirtschaft*. Retrieved September 12, 2008, from bmu.de/atomenergie/ausstieg_atom energie/doc /2715.php Available as PDF at bmu.de/files/pdfs/allgemein/application/pdf/akw_faq.pdf

141. Sarah van Gelder. 2008. "13 Best Energy Ideas." Retrieved on July 17, 2008, from yesmagazine.org/article. asp?ID=2280

142. Marc Gunther. October 4, 2007. "For solar power, the future looks bright." *Fortune*. Retrieved October 17, 2007, from money.cnn.com/2007/10/03/news/companies/sunpower_solar. fortune/index.htm

143. Berkeley Mayor's Office. February 27, 2008. "Berkeley FIRST: Financing Initiative for Renewable and Solar Technology — FAQ." Retrieved June 24, 2008, from ci.berkeley. ca.us/mayor//GHG/SEFD-FAQ.htm

144. Carolyn Jones. October 26, 2007. "Berkeley going solar: city pays up front, recoups over 20 years. *San Francisco Chronicle*. Retrieved June 24, 2008, from sfgate.com/cgi-bin/article.cgi?f=/c/a/2007/10/26/MNAIT0DQO.DTL

145. Northern California Solar Energy Association. 2008. "Berkeley FIRST: Financing Initiative for Solar and Renewable Technology." Retrieved September 25, 2008, from norcalsolar. org/index.php?option=com_content& task=view&id=93&Itemid=26

146. City of Berkeley. 2008. "Climate Action Plan January 2008: DRAFT for Public Review and Comment." Available at berkeleyclimate action.org/docManager/1000000121/CAP_Final.pdf

147. City of Berkeley. June 7, 1983. "Resolution No. 55,813 - N.S.: Adopting a Local Business Preference Program for Purchases of Supplies and Non-professional Services." Available at cityofberkeley.info/uploadedFiles/Planning _and_Development/Level_3_Energy _and_Sustainable_Development/Local %20Business%20Preference.pdf

148. City of Berkeley. May 1, 1990. "Resolution No. 55,327 - N.S.: Adopting the Policy That the City Has a Preference for Purchasing Recycled Paper and That White Paper be Utilized for Office Use and Related Activities." Available at cityofberkeley.info/uploaded Files/Planning_and_Development/Level_ 3_-Energy_and_Sustainable_Development /Purchasing%20Recycled%20Paper.pdf

149. City of Berkeley. October 14, 2003. "Resolution No. 62,259 - N.S.: Adopt the 'Precautionary Principle' and Refer to Staff the Development of a Precautionary Principle Ordinance to Inform Decisions on Public Health, the Environment, Natural Resources, Sustainability, and Quality of Life."

Available at cityofberkeley.info/uploaded Files/Planning_and_Development/Level _3_Energy_and_Sustainable_Develop ment/Precautionary%20Principle(1).pdf

150. City of Berkeley. October 19, 2004. "Resolution No. 62,693 - N.S: Adopting an Environmentally Preferable Purchasing Policy (EPP)." Available at cityofberkeley.info/uploaded Files/Planning_and_Development/Level _3_-_Energy_and_Sustainable_ Development/Environmental%20Prefer able%20Puchasing%20Resolution.pdf.

151. City of Berkeley. April 20, 2006. "Ordinance No. 6,911 - N.S.: Adding Berkeley Municipal Code Chapter 12.29, Precautionary Principle." Available at cityofberkeley.info/uploaded Files/Planning_and_Development/Level _3_Energy_and_Sustainable_Develop ment/Precautionary%20Principle.pdf

152. City of Berkeley. November 18, 2003. "Resolution No. 62,284 - N.S.: Adopting Policies and Actions Requiring the Use of the United States Green Building Council's LEED® (Leadership in Energy and Environmental Design) Green Building Ratings System Standards for City Owned and Operated Projects." Available at cityofberkeley.info/uploaded Files/Planning_and_Development/Level _3_Energy_and_Sustainable_Develop ment/Green%20Building(3).pdf

153. City of Berkeley. January 18, 2005. "Resolution No. 62,738 - N.S.: Endorsing the Kyoto Protocol Calling for the Reduction of Greenhouse Emissions and Urging the U.S. government to Join Most of the Other Nations of the World in Their Commitment to Reduce Emissions to Address the Threat Posed by Global Warming." Available at cityofberkeley.info/uploadedFiles/Plan ning_and_Development/Level_3_Energy _and_Sustainable_Development/Kyoto %20Protocol%20Endorsement.pdf

154. City of Berkeley. March 22, 2005. "Resolution No. 62,849 - N.S.: Reaffirming the City's Zero Waste Goal and Referring the Issue to the Solid Waste Commission." Available at cityof berkeley.info/uploadedFiles/Planning_ and_Development/Level_3_Energy_and _Sustainable_Development/Zero%20 Waste%20Goal.pdf

155. Bundesministerium für Umwelt, Naturschutz und Reaktorsicherheit. 2008. "Fragen und Antworten zum Wärmegesetz." Retrieved September 13, 2008, from erneuerbare-energien.de/ inhalt/40704/

156. BBC. November 3, 2008. "Prince calls for rainforest bills." Retrieved November 4, 2008, from news.bbc.co.uk/2/hi/asia-pacific/ 7705826.stm

157. Amory B. Lovins and Hunter Lovins. 1991. *Least-Cost Climatic Stabilization*. Rocky Mountain Institute. Available free from rmi.org/images/other/Energy/E91- 33_LstCostClimateStabli.pdf

158. Hammarby Sjöstad. 2007. "Hammarby Sjöstad: a new city district with emphasis on water and ecology." Available at hammarbysjostad.se/inenglish /pdf/Folder_komb_eng_2007 1026.pdf

159. Hammarby Sjöstad. 2008. "Environmental Goals: energy." Retrieved April 25, 2008, from hammarbysjostad.se /frameset.asp?target=inenglish/inengli sh_goals_energy.asp

160. Hammarby Sjöstad. 2007. "Hammarby Sjöstad: a unique environmental project in Stockholm. Available at hammarbysjostad.se/inenglish/pdf/HS _miljo_bok_eng_ny.pdf

161. Hammarby Sjöstad. 2008. "Environmental Goals: waste." Retrieved April 25, 2008, from hammarbysjostad .se/frameset.asp?target=inenglish/inengli sh_goals_waste.asp

162. Swedish Trade Council. 2008. "Waste." Retrieved November 2, 2008, from symbiocity.org/?pageId=27

163. Institute for Local Self-Reliance. 2006. "Zero Waste Planning." Retrieved November 6, 2008, from ilsr.org/recycling/zerowaste/index.html

164. Växjö kommun. 2004. "Fossil Fuel Free Växjö." Available at sustainablecommunities.fcm. ca/files/Program _Docs/2004_Sweden_Mission/fos-fuel-free-_Vaxjo.pdf

165. Robert E. Lane. 2001. *The Loss of Happiness in Market Democracies.* Yale University Press.

166. Mark Anielski. 2007. *The Economics of Happiness: Building Genuine Wealth.* New Society Publishers.

167. T.J. Keefe. 2007. "The nature of light." Retrieved June 24, 2008, from ccri.edu/physics/keefe/light.htm

Multiplying stated conversion efficiencies of electrical power conversion of incandescent light bulbs to visible light with typical power plant efficiencies of converting primary fossil fuel energy to end-user electricity, e.g. 40%, yields overall system efficiency.

168. Royal Dutch Shell. 2003. "World-Beating Eco-Car Delivers 10,705 mpg: French Students Beat Own World Record at UK Eco-Marathon." *Impact,* No. 4, 2003: 8. Retrieved May 19, 2004, from shell globalsolutions.com. Link expired. The eco-car uses less than 0.21% of the energy of a car with average US fleet efficiency of 23 miles/gallon (10.2 l/100 km) for a single occupant moving at 20 to 25 miles/hour (30 to 40 km/h).

169. Godo Stoyke. 2007. *The Carbon Buster's Home Energy Handbook: Slowing Climate Change and Saving Money.* New Society Publishers.

170. Wikipedia. November 12, 2008. "German armored fighting vehicle production during World War II." Retrieved December 19, 2008, from en.wikipedia.org/wiki/German_armored _fighting_vehicle_production_during _World_War_II

171. Wikipedia. October 28, 2008. "American armored fighting vehicle production during World War II." Retrieved December 19, 2008, from en.wikipedia.org/wiki/American_armored _fighting_vehicle_production_during _World_War_II

172. Doris Kearns Goodwin. 1994. *No Ordinary Time.* Simon and Schuster: 313.

173. ICLEI. 2008. "About ICLEI." Retrieved September 29, 2008, from iclei.org/index.php?id=global-about -iclei

174. Paul Gipe, July 9, 2008. "Tables of Renewable Tariffs or Feed-In Tariffs Worldwide." Retrieved September 27, 2008, from windworks.org/Feed Laws/TableofRenewableTariffsorFeed-InTariffsWorldwide.html

175. Paul Hawken, Amory Lovins, and L. Hunter Lovins. 1999. *Natural Capitalism.* Little, Brown and Company.

176. Carbon Busters calculations, March 30, 2009. Assumptions: Baseload energy consumption (including negawatts) increases at the historical rate of 2003 to 2007 (0.828 Quadrillion BTU per year). Negawatts deliver 75% of energy needs. Nuclear stations are shut down as their 40 year initial licenses expires. The remaining energy needs are met entirely by renewables. Historic consumption (2003-2007) from Energy Information Administration. May 2008. U.S. Energy Consumption by Energy Source. Retrieved March 29, 2009 from eia.doe.gov/cneaf/alternate/ page/renew_energy_consump/table1 .html. Nuclear data from Energy Information Administration. 2009.

U.S. Nuclear Reactors. Retrieved March 30, 2009 from eia.doe.gov/cneaf/nuclear/page/nuc_reactors/reactsum.html.

177. Carbon Busters calculations, April 3, 2009, based on an 83% reduction in fuel consumption of light-duty vehicles (LDV) from two- to sixfold increases of fuel efficiency (depending on vehicle type), increased use of public transit and bicycles, and new categories of alternative vehicles ranging from electric bikes and Segway-type modes of transportation to ultra-efficient single-passenger transport vehicles (USTVs), a further 90% LDV fuel consumption reduction through conversion to renewable electricity use in PHEV and electric vehicles, a 7% increase in long-haul truck efficiency through hybrids, 20% reduction in local driving truck fuel consumption through hybrid and PHEV technology, long-distance trucking reduction of 50% through more localized economies and train use, a 25% reduction in airline fuel use through the increased use of high-speed trains and continued fuel efficiency gains in airplane design, a 20% reduction in asphalt requirements due to reduced road construction and better utilization of existing roads through public transit, a 30% reduction in shipping fuel use through more efficient ship design, including high-tech kite technology and more localized economies, a 50% reduction in industrial petroleum feedstock use through reduced waste, increased waste recovery and dematerialization, and a 90% reduction in building energy fuel use through adoption of passive house and zero-carbon building designs and retrofits. To reduce carbon emissions of electricity use in this scenario the conversion of our electrical grid to renewable sources has to proceed simultaneously to the increases in efficiency.

178. Carbon Busters calculations, April 5, 2009, based on 7 kWh energy content per liter of biofuel, average annual production of 1 kWh per installed Watt of photovoltaics, 6.75 gigaWatt-hours per year for each 2 MW wind turbine, and a 10% conversion of the current square footage of US national building stock.

INDEX

ABOUT THE AUTHOR

GODO STOYKE IS AN award-winning environmental researcher and presenter with a Master of Science degree from the University of Alberta. Godo is president of Carbon Busters (carbonbusters.org), a sustainability consultancy focusing on energy efficiency and green and zero carbon design. Carbon Busters has saved institutional and commercial clients over 150 million pounds of CO_2 and over US$20 million in utility bills. Godo has been living in an off-grid solar powered home near Edmonton, Alberta for the last 19 years with his wife Shanthu and son Calan. He is currently designing a zero carbon community near Edmonton, Alberta, featuring 256 zero carbon homes and businesses, a green business incubator, community food infrastructure, innovative systems for water conservation, and community green transportation systems. Godo was selected as one of 50 green Canadians making a difference by *Green Living Magazine* in 2008.

If you have enjoyed *The Carbon Charter*, you might also enjoy other

BOOKS TO BUILD A NEW SOCIETY

Our books provide positive solutions for people who want to make a difference. We specialize in:

Sustainable Living • Ecological Design and Planning
Natural Building & Appropriate Technology
Environment and Justice • Conscientious Commerce
Progressive Leadership • Resistance and Community • Nonviolence
Educational and Parenting Resources

New Society Publishers

ENVIRONMENTAL BENEFITS STATEMENT

New Society Publishers has chosen to produce this book on recycled paper made with 100% post consumer waste, processed chlorine free, and old growth free.

For every 5,000 books printed, New Society saves the following resources:[1]

15	Trees
1,338	Pounds of Solid Waste
1,472	Gallons of Water
1,920	Kilowatt Hours of Electricity
2,431	Pounds of Greenhouse Gases
10	Pounds of HAPs, VOCs, and AOX Combined
4	Cubic Yards of Landfill Space

[1]Environmental benefits are calculated based on research done by the Environmental Defense Fund and other members of the Paper Task Force who study the environmental impacts of the paper industry.

For a full list of NSP's titles, please call 1-800-567-6772 or check out our web site at:

www.newsociety.com

NEW SOCIETY PUBLISHERS